T0144504

Innovating with Augmented Reality

Innovating with Augmented Reality

Applications in Education and Industry

Edited by
P. Kaliraj
T. Devi

CRC Press
Taylor & Francis Group
Boca Raton London New York

CRC Press is an imprint of the
Taylor & Francis Group, an **informa** business

AN AUERBACH BOOK

First Edition published 2022
by CRC Press
6000 Broken Sound Parkway NW, Suite 300, Boca Raton, FL 33487-2742

and by CRC Press
2 Park Square, Milton Park, Abingdon, Oxon, OX14 4RN

© 2022 Taylor & Francis Group, LLC

CRC Press is an imprint of Taylor & Francis Group, LLC

Library of Congress Cataloging-in-Publication Data
A catalog record has been requested for this book

ISBN: 978-1-032-00812-7 (hbk)
ISBN: 978-1-032-15119-9 (pbk)
ISBN: 978-1-003-17589-6 (ebk)

DOI: 10.1201/9781003175896

Typeset in Garamond
by MPS Limited, Dehradun

Contents

Preface

The world today has seen a massive change in manufacturing since the adoption of Industry 4.0, which comprises smart factories, cognitive computing, cloud computing, augmented reality (AR), Internet of Things, and cyber-physical systems. The industrial revolutions Industry 4.0 and Industry 5.0 are changing the world around us. Improved collaboration is seen between smart systems and humans, which merges the critical and cognitive thinking abilities of humans with highly accurate and fast industrial automation.

AR provides the experience of an augmented world to users by overlaying virtual information in the real world. AR is an interactive experience of a real-world environment where the objects in the real world are enhanced by computer-generated perceptual information, sometimes across multiple sensory modalities, including visual, auditory, haptic, somatosensory and olfactory. The advantage is that the user can be in touch with both the physical world and the virtual world and thus obtain real-time data and statistics.

The fourth and fifth industrial revolutions affect the roles that Indian universities and colleges prepare students for, and educational institutions are committed to helping produce the workforce for this new world and the student experience to match it. It is necessary to align higher education with Industry 4.0 through education on the tools of Industry 4.0. As a tool of Industry 4.0, students should be made familiar with AR and learn how to apply AR techniques in the domains they work. This book discusses AR and how it is used in specific application areas.

Bharathiar University has designed guidelines for Curriculum 4.0 and has prepared new syllabi for all subjects intertwining Industry 4.0 and 5.0 tools onto various disciplines, such as science, social science, arts, and education. The University has identified the gap in knowledge resources, such as books, course materials, interdisciplinary curricula, and innovative programs. To fill this gap and to prepare the future pillars of our globe to face the volatile, uncertain, complex, and ambiguous world, and to help the academic community, Bharathiar University has prepared guidelines for revising the syllabus, designing innovative faculty development programs, establishing connectivity to the real world for students, incubating creativity, and inculcating design thinking. Moreover, with the active participation of all stakeholders under the esteemed leadership of the Honourable Vice-Chancellor, Prof. P. Kaliraj, interdisciplinary books are being edited for Education 4.0 and 5.0.

AR has many advantages, including increased engagement and interaction, enhanced innovation and responsiveness, easy accessibility to the smartphone market, and cost-effectiveness. This technology is found to have applications in almost all domains, such as medical training, retail, repair and maintenance of complex equipment such as car motors or MRI machines, interior design for architecture and construction, business logistics, virtual "walkabouts" for potential tourists, classroom education, laboratory practicals, and field service, to build deeper bonds between characters and the audience in the entertainment field, and to provide geolocation-enabled AR for public safety. This book in this context will uncover the details behind this technology, explore some of its application areas, and explore how this technology gets aligned with Education 4.0.

AR applications can provide a new level of interactive experiences and thus improved information. Companies are now leveraging this technology to provide their customers with the ability to experience their products' firsthand information and experience. Suppose typical apps on smartphones simply drove customers to the market. In that case, their counterpart AR apps allow users to visually experience the products by allowing them to deeply engage with the products as if they have already bought them. AR applications enable unique opportunities for immersive reality when sharing locations and places through social networks. AR applications can complement a standard curriculum by superimposing text, graphics, audio, and video into a student's real-time environment even in the educational domain. Thus, there are a lot of promising and exciting advantages when AR is brought to common use.

As per an estimate by Goldman Sachs, AR and virtual reality (VR) are expected to grow into a $95 billion market by 2025. There is a great need for educated individuals who have expertise in this domain. And with the demand for talented professionals more than doubling in the last few years, there are limitless opportunities for professionals who want to work on the cutting edge of AR application development. Universities and higher education institutions need to offer a prescribed set of courses for a major or specialization in AR, while those with dedicated AR programs may have unique approaches to the discipline. This will create graduates who are skilled in AR, and this book can help impart the concepts and knowledge of AR to graduates. This book provides a blend of the fundamentals and applications of AR with the description of its fundamentals, tools, challenges, and subfields of AR. This book on AR provides relevant theory and industrial applications of AR in various domains such as the beverage industry, education, gaming, and healthcare.

What's in the Book?

AR is the topic of discussion for this book, which comprises eight chapters. These chapters give exclusive understanding and exposure to the world of AR, with real-time examples and applications to provide a strong theoretical grip on this technology.

Starting with a discussion of a solid foundation for this technology, the chapters make available some application areas of this emerging domain. Due to the rapid advancements in technology, it is necessary that the future education system must prepare future graduates to be ready to work with the latest technologies by enabling them to learn virtually in augmented ways in varied platforms. By providing an illusion of physical objects, which takes the students to a new world of imagination, AR and VR create virtual and interactive environments for better learning and understanding. Hence, education is an application area that is dealt with in four chapters of this book. How gamification can be used in the teaching and learning process is covered in one chapter. Another application area dealt with in this section is the food and beverage industry with case studies on virtual 3D food, employee training, product–customer interaction, restaurant entertainment, restaurant tours, and product packaging.

One chapter familiarizes the reader with game development software, Unity, a real-time development platform for 2D and 3D AR and VR. A chapter on app development opens up details on the software, libraries, and techniques available for app development. The application of AR in the healthcare sector, medical education, and related gadgets and software are described in the last chapter.

Chapter 1, entitled *Augmented Reality,* provides an exclusive understanding and exposure to the world of AR with real-time examples and gives a solid theoretical grip on AR by providing a 360-degree view of the world of AR.

Chapter 2, entitled *Industry 4.0: Augmented and Virtual Reality in Education,* provides insight into the emerging technologies – AR and VR – that will create a virtual and interactive environment for better understanding in various sectors. The AR and VR technology thus provide an illusion of the presence of physical objects and take users to a new world of imagination. This chapter also discusses the basic concepts of AR and VR, types, hardware and software requirements, and applications of AR and VR technology in various areas, especially in education and industries.

Chapter 3, entitled *Augmented Reality Changing the Food and Beverage Industries,* discusses the revolution made by AR in the food and beverage industries. Applications of AR in various sectors of the industry that includes virtual 3D food, product–customer interaction, restaurant entertainment, employee training, restaurant tours, and food packaging are discussed. Also, technologies used and their impact on the industry are discussed. Finally, the chapter concludes with the future of food.

Chapter 4, entitled *Augmented Reality: A Boon for the Teaching and Learning Process,* enlightens how AR accelerates teaching and learning by using different applications of AR. It describes the history of AR, recent development of AR, elements of AR, place and benefits of AR, experiences in an AR classroom, role of AR in the teaching and learning process, the impact of AR, using AR for learners' development, applications of AR and the need for resources in the classroom, the future of AR in education, and three-dimensional learning models. Simplifying learning and teaching by using AR is clearly shown in this chapter.

Chapter 5, entitled *New Horizons for Learning: Augmented Reality in Education,* details AR technology and its educational potential. New technologies in education include smart classrooms for subject deliverance, webcast lectures, open educational resources (OER), video and interactive video tutorials, AR, virtual labs, VR, personalization, blended learning, individualized learning using portable devices, flipped learning, MOOCS, SPOC, mobile learning (M-learning), gamification, cloud-based learning, artificial intelligence, chat bots, Internet of Things, and big data, which are slowly finding their way into educational institutions. Fundamental techniques and methods are discussed in the context of education.

Chapter 6, entitled *Gamification for Education 5.0,* describes AR games that can change learning for students. Some of the popular tools for gamification for math programs, language learning, and classroom platforms that can be adapted to all platforms are detailed. The case studies of using gamification in school education for music, biology, mathematics, literacy, and vocabulary learning, and in higher education for information studies, computer science, computer organization and cloud computing, library, UML, mathematics, vocational courses, factory management, manufacturing training, software development, French language, and software engineering are given with the features used and the results. Finally, the effects of gamification on their satisfaction, cognitive load, and social problems are described.

Chapter 7, entitled *Augmented Reality Apps: A Developer's Perception,* describes a perception of a developer who is into creating applications that employ the use of newer emerging technology, AR. The chapter describes what AR is all about, differences between AR and VR, rules/constraints that need to be followed, libraries available for developers to develop applications, technical concepts associated with AR, use cases and, finally, a no-code approach for application development which can be installed on any smartphone independent of the operating system they are functioning on to understand what Augmented Reality actually means.

Chapter 8, entitled *Modernized Healthcare Using Augmented Reality,* details the applications of AR in healthcare and case studies on medical education, nurse training, dentistry, surgical visualization, and diagnostic imaging. Technologies that include gadgets and software packages behind augmented reality are described.

How to Use the Book

The method and purpose of using this book depend on the role that you play in an educational institution or an industry or depend on the focus of your interest. We propose five types of roles: student, software developer, teacher, member of Board of Studies, and researcher.

If you are a student: Students can use the book to get a basic understanding of augmented reality, its tools and applications. Students belonging to any of the arts, science, education, and social science disciplines will find useful information from chapters on *Augmented Reality* and *Industry 4.0: Augmented and Virtual Reality in Education.* This book will serve as a starting point for beginners. Students will benefit from the chapters on applications of AR in education – teaching and learning, food and beverage industries, entertainment (gamification) and healthcare.

If you are a software or mobile app developer. Software or mobile app developers can use the book to get a basic understanding of AR, its tools and applications. Readers with a software development background will find useful information from the chapter on *Augmented Reality Apps: A Developer's Perception.* They will also benefit from the chapters on education – teaching and learning, gamification and healthcare.

If you are a teacher. The book is useful as a text for several different university and college-level undergraduate and postgraduate courses. A graduate course on augmented reality can use this book as a primary textbook. It is important to equip the learners with a basic understanding on AR as a tool of Industry 4.0. Chapters on *Augmented Reality* and *Industry 4.0: Augmented and Virtual Reality in Education* provide the fundamentals of AR. To teach the applications of AR in various sectors such as Education, Healthcare, Food and Beverages, teachers will find useful information from this book. A course on AR and its applications could also use the chapters in this book.

If you are a member of the Board of Studies: Innovating the education to align with Industry 4.0 requires that the curriculum be revisited. Universities are looking for methods of incorporating Industry 4.0 tools across various disciplines of Arts, Science, Education and Social Science. This book helps in incorporating AR across Science, Education and Entertainment. The book is useful while framing the syllabus for new courses that cut across AR and disciplines of Arts or Science Education. For example, syllabi for courses entitled augmented reality in science, augmented reality in education, or augmented reality in healthcare may be framed using the chapters in the book. Industry infusion into curriculum is given much importance by involving more industry experts – R&D managers, product development managers, and technical managers – as special invitees in the Board of Studies. Chapters given by industrial experts in this book will help infuse the application part of augmented reality into the curriculum.

If you are a researcher. A crucial area where innovation is required is the research work carried out by universities and institutions so that innovative, creative and valuable products and services are made available to society through translational research. This book can serve as a comprehensive reference guide for researchers in developing experimental AR applications and mobile apps. The chapters on *Augmented Reality Changing Food and Beverage Industries, Augmented Reality: A Boon for Teaching and Learning Process, New Horizons for Learning: Augmented Reality in Education, Gamification for Education 5.0, and Modernized Healthcare Using Augmented Reality* provide researchers, scholars, and students a base for research in the area of AR.

Acknowledgments

From Prof. P. Kaliraj

First and foremost, I express my sincere gratitude to **Hon'ble Shri. Banwarilal Purohit,** Governor of Tamil Nadu, India, who was instrumental in organizing the conference on Innovating Education in the Era of Industry 4.0 during 14–15 December 2019 in Ooty, which paved the way for further work in Industry 4.0 world knowledge.

My heartfelt thanks go to Hon'ble Chief Minister of Tamil Nadu, India, and Hon'ble Minister for Higher Education, Government of Tamil Nadu. I thank Principal Secretary to Government, Higher Education Department, Government of Tamil Nadu.

I would like to express my thanks to Secretary to Governor, and Deputy Secretary to Governor, Universities Governor's Secretariat, Raj Bhavan, Chennai.

I thank my wife Dr. Vanaja Kaliraj and family members for supporting me and being patient.

From Prof. T. Devi

I record my sincere thanks to **Prof. P. Kaliraj**, Hon'ble Vice-Chancellor of Bharathiar University, who identified the gap in the knowledge world when Professor searched for a book on Industry 4.0 and triggered the process of writing and editing books in the Industry 4.0 series. His continuous motivation during the lockdown period due to COVID-19, sensitization, and encouragement are unmatchable.

I express my profound thanks to the Vice-Chancellor and Registrar for administrative support. Heartfelt thanks are due to the authors of the chapters for their contribution of chapters, continuous co-operation in improvising the chapters as and when requested, and for timely communication. I thank all the expert members who served as reviewers for providing quality and swift reviews.

We wish to thank **Mr. John Wyzalek, Senior Acquisitions Editor, Taylor & Francis/CRC Press,** who believed in the idea of this book and helped us in realizing our dream.

Special thanks are due to Ms. Stephanie Kiefer, editorial assistant, and Mr. Todd Perry, production editor, Taylor & Francis Group/CRC Press, for their excellent coordination and Mr. Manmohan Negi, Project Manager, MPS Ltd., for his untiring and swift support.

Thanks are due to Dr. R. Rajeswari, Associate Professor, Department of Computer Applications, for her continuous support; as well as to Sister Italia Joseph Maria, Ms. M. Lissa, Mrs. Shalini, Project Assistants, for providing earnest support.

Thanks to the faculty members Prof. M. Punithavalli, Dr. T. Amudha, Dr. J. Satheeshkumar, Dr. V. Bhuvaneswari, Dr. R. Balu, and Dr. J. Ramsingh.

Thanks to the Assistant Technical Officers Mr. A. Elanchezian, Mr. A. Sivaraj, and Mrs. B. Priyadarshini and office staff Mr. A. Kalidas of the Department of Computer Applications of Bharathiar University, India.

Thanks are due to Mrs. K. Kowsalya, Assistant Registrar; Mr. R. Karthick, Assistant Section Officer; and Mr. A. Prasanth of the Office of the Vice-Chancellor and staff of the Office of the Registrar of Bharathiar University, India.

Finally, I thank my husband Mr. D. Ravi, daughter Mrs. R. Deepiga, son Mr. R. Surya, son-in-law Mr. D. Vishnu Prakhash and grandson V. Deera and family members for their encouragement and support.

*****

Editors

Prof. P. Kaliraj, Hon'ble Vice-Chancellor, Bharathiar University, a Visionary and an Eminent Leader leading big academic teams, has more than three decades of teaching and research experience. He has held various renowned positions, such as officiating Vice-Chancellor of Anna University, Head of Centre for Biotechnology of Anna University, Dean of Faculty at A C College of Technology, and Member of the Syndicate for two decades at Anna University. Professor Kaliraj had research collaborations with the National Institute of Health in Maryland, USA; Glasgow University in Scotland, UK; and University of Illinois in Rockford, USA. He received the University Grants Commission BSR Faculty Award and the Lifetime Achievement Award from the Biotechnology Research Society of India. **Forty-two scholars were gifted to receive the highest academic degree under his distinguished guidance.** His remarkable **patent in the area of Filariasis is a boon in healthcare** and saving the lives of mankind. He is a great motivator and very good at sensitizing the faculty, scholars, and students towards achieving academic excellence and institutional global ranking. Professor Kaliraj a recipient of the **Life Time Achievement Award and Sir J.C. Bose Memorial Award** for his Outstanding Contribution in Higher Education – Research. (email: vc@buc.edu.in, pkaliraj@gmail.com)

Prof. T. Devi Ph.D. (UK), Professor of Research and Evaluation, Professor and Head, Department of Computer Applications, Bharathiar University, focuses on state-of-art technology that industries adopt in order to make the students ready for the future world. She is a **Gold Medalist** (1981–1984) from University of Madras and a **Commonwealth Scholar** (1994–1998) for her **Ph.D. from University of Warwick, UK.** She has three decades of teaching and research experience from Bharathiar University, Indian Institute of Foreign Trade, New Delhi, and University of Warwick, UK. Professor Devi is good in team building and setting goals and achieving. Her research interests include integrated data modeling and frameworks, meta-modeling, computer-assisted concurrent engineering, and speech processing. Professor Devi visited the UK, Tanzania, and Singapore for academic collaborations. She has received various awards, including the **Commonwealth Scholarship and Best Alumni Award from PSGR Krishnammal College for Women (PSGRKCW), Proficiency award from PSG College of Technology and awards from Bharathiar University for serving for BU-NIRF, Curriculum 4.0, and Roadmap 2030 and guided 23 Ph.D. scholars.** (email: tdevi@buc.edu.in, tdevi5@gmail.com)

Contributors

A. Aravind
Department of Mechanical Engineering
Sree Vidyanikethan Engineering College
Tirupati, India

R. Balaji
Hardware enthusiast
Sri Ramakrishna Engineering College
Coimbatore, India

P. Bhanu Prasad
Advisor to R&D Centres
France, Germany, and India

V. Bhuvaneswari
Department of Computer Applications
Bharathiar University
Coimbatore, India

P. Janardhana Kumar Reddy
Department of Education
Bharathiar University
Coimbatore, India

D. Kalaivani
Department of Information Science and
    Engineering
New Horizon College of Engineering
Bengaluru, India

M. Lissa
Department of Computer Applications
Bharathiar University
Coimbatore, India

N. Padmaja
Sree Vidyanikethan Engineering College
Tirupati, India

Bhanu Prasad
Advisor to R&D Centres
France, Germany, and India

D. Ramya Chitra
Department of Computer Science
Bharathiar University
Coimbatore, India

P. Ranjit Jeba Thangaiah
Karunya Institute of Technology and
    Sciences
Coimbatore, India

B. Satish Kumar
Department of ECE
Sree Vidyanikethan Engineering College
Tirupati, India

G. Singaravelu
Department of Education
Bharathiar University
Coimbatore, India

N.S. Sukanya
Bharathiar University
Coimbatore, India

Chapter 1

Augmented Reality

M. Lissa[1] and V. Bhuvaneswari[2]

[1]*Ph.D. Research Scholar, Department of Computer Applications, Bharathiar University, Coimbatore, India*
[2]*Associate Professor, Department of Computer Applications, Bharathiar University, Coimbatore, India*

Contents

DOI: 10.1201/9781003175896-1

Objective

The main objective of this chapter is to focus on giving immense knowledge about emerged technology Augmented Reality, and it is essential to have a base knowledge about the technology before plunging into the field of experiencing. The chapter has five sections to give exclusive understanding and exposure to the world of Augmented Reality. It provides a 360-degree view of the world of AR and explains with real-time examples the variety of aspects that can be developed through Augmented Reality technology. It will provide a solid theoretical grip on the AR and a brief overview of the world of AR for underlying developments. The chapter also provides a holistic approach and concise overview of the realm of AR and how the world is being adopted by it day in and day out. AR cannot be categorized as a simple technology, but rather a combination of set of technological innovations.

1.1 Introduction to Augmented Reality

The chapter introduces Augmented Reality for the students and the people who are looking forward to learning more about emerging technologies this covers the core concepts which involve basics, features, advantages, tools, and technologies of Augmented Reality with real-time applications. The basic history and the term Augmented Reality is commonly abbreviated as AR, which emerged in the year 1992 by two airplane engineers of Boeing Thoman and David. The first experiment and goal are to create a display that can transform the physical world that is replacing the real world with digital reality. It needs more complex programmatical codes and big suspended machines, and mechanical arms to display (Craig, 2013).

Today there is no longer a need for heavy machines instead of the independent hardware referred to as standalone headsets or head-mounted display. In short, it is called an HMD this is also an AR content delivery system first introduced by the Microsoft Hololens, it is a wireless and rechargeable battery present within a frame. On the other side, the smartphone development industry contributed to AR's growth because the components used for AR are the same for mobile devices. Also, AR is created using face and rear camera on smartphones by holding it up the screen can display digital objects and information integrated within the real world. Now the smartphone itself can act as a portal to a new world's experience and knowledge.

AR begins with the most powerful and broadly applicable matters, as was the Internet itself. It is self – an evident and eventual conclusion reached when anyone, achieving upon a basic level of comprehension, spends a few moments considering the limitless potential that augmented reality promises. Spatial and interactive were AR builds on what has come before and takes connectedness to new places and it is a medium that allows you to interact with digital data visually and spatially that is utterly seamless with your environment and everyday life.

1.1.1 Definition and Augmented Reality Characteristics

The technology involved in Augmented Reality can project 3D models directly or insert, fuse, and overlay digital and virtual information in the real-world environment. AR can be leveraged to recognize things and see things and get instantaneous information via a Smartphone. In AR, the images generated by the computer are superimposed on the physical world which changes the perception of reality. AR projects a real-world environment by adding sounds, videos, or graphics to it that helps to experience an automated tour with audio Augmented Reality (Bederson, 1995).

The characteristics that define Augmented Reality are related to interactive concepts which include combining the real and virtual world, the virtual environment created with the AR experience is interactive. The real images and virtual images are combined and can be seen at the same time. 3D objects appear in a fixed space where it is spatially registered AR, it also makes simple interaction.

Focuses on the main three characteristics

a. Integration with a real-world environment
b. Real-time integration
c. Alignment in the 3D model to embed in the focused area

1.1.2 Difference between Augmented Reality and Virtual Reality

Virtual reality is defined as the use of computer technology to create a simulated environment, it makes the users immerse into the environment and interact with the 3D worlds. Virtual Reality simulates the various senses like vision, touch, hearings, a smell which transforms to experience the artificial world. It creates an artificial environment to experience the 3D world on the other phase augmented reality helps to simulate the artificial objects in the real environment. A brief comparison of Augmented Reality and Virtual Reality is explained as shown in Table 1.1.

1.1.3 Current Industry Landscape

AR technologies produce a digital immersive user experience across various industry verticals like Gaming, Entertainment, Media, Aerospace, Healthcare,

Table 1.1 Augmented Reality vs. Virtual Reality

Augmented Reality	Virtual Reality
The digital elements can be added to the actual environment by using Augmented Reality (AR) (Hubspot, 2018)	The user can interact with the virtual world which does not exist and get an immersive experience with the use of Virtual Reality (VR) (Hubspot, 2018)
Augmented Reality is a live direct or indirect view of a physical world environment whose elements are augmented by computer-generated or extracted real-world sensory (Geospatial, 2018)	The real world fits with virtual objects with Virtual Reality used in headsets, sometimes in combination with physical space (Geospatial, 2018)
AR supplements the world with digital objects of any sort, Airplane pilot helmets that display data within the pilot's view as they fly are AR headsets (Geospatial, 2018)	Multi projected environments to generate realistic images, VR devices are Facebook's Oculus, Samsung's gear or Google Cardboard are all VR devices (Geospatial, 2018)

Education, Manufacturing, Retail, and others. The key market players are Alphabet (Google Inc.), DAQRI, Facebook, HTC, Magic Leap, Inc., Microsoft Corporation, Osterhout Design Group, Samsung Electronics Co., Ltd, Sony, Wikitude (Prnewswire, 2020). As per the statistics (Tech Jury, 2019) of finance, online reviews for the business world population are access to AR technology via Facebook, Snapchat, and many graphic software solutions that adapt to this technology by applying AR elements for realistic rendering (Financesonline.com, 2020). More than twenty industry giants make AR products for consumers to benefit in the part of product demonstrations, workplace training, and workplace safety (Tech Jury, 2019). Among all the technology giants, main market players for AR gains competitiveness to increase the sales of AR smart glasses, and they are dominant market players Google LLC (Alphabet INC.), Seiko Epson Corporation, Vuzik Corporation, RealWear Inc., Toshiba Corporation, and Vuforia (Mordorintelligence.co., 2020). The statistics of International Data Corporation (IDC) for the global market of the Information technology industry is categorized into four divisions as software, Device and Infrastructure, Business services, Emerging technologies, Telecommunication services (Azuma, 1997). A part of this division is to focus on emerging technologies that show 46 percent as per the survey (Olsson & Salo, 2011) of the share is sourced among the global market it is significantly higher than other global regions. The industry invests in software services mainly to provide a robust infrastructure and platform by enabling devices communication through the service of software so it paves the way for emerging technologies that drive the growth of global revenue. The automobile industry widely uses this technology for designing and structuring the body of the vehicle it is estimated that automotive companies depict the immense pockets of investment. As part of emerging technological growth drivers, Augmented Reality is one of the other technology sectors. The Industry landscape rapidly changes with the digital transformation, which provides new skills and values to apply in modern business and society with technology.

1.1.3.1 AR Today

The current state of AR applications transforms the smartphone's use in different views by using a marker that is connected with digital animation or the phone pinpoints the location with the help of GPS, the real-time experience happens with the augmentation and within the context of the environment. Technology plays a major role in marketing medium, a popular giant in the industry called IKEA created an AR application designed the catalog which populates the three-dimensional model in various pages with a camera in the application to visualize the product.

As it seems to be revolutionary, real-world applications create heads up applications for pilots, and the great pioneer among the car brands BMW uses the features of augmented reality by displaying information such as speed, navigation and injects it from the console on the dashboard on the glass which can be viewed only who drives the car. Various types of applications are developed today like Projection-based AR which projects it with synthetic lights as in the hologram of Microsoft, Superimposition-based AR replaces it with the virtual item. Augmented Reality emerged as a key driver of the technological economy because of AR headsets, Smart glasses, and AR applications as per the global economy prediction this makes a big impact in the field of education and across the broad. In the Health field, students practicing medicine broadly make use of AR headsets to experience and delve into the human body with digital 3D models. E-Commerce uses more to advertise and demonstrate the products to the user's choice by customizing the colors and features using AR applications. Architect modelers and constructors make use of Augmented Reality to visualize the final product in the period of creation, engineers use AR headsets to visualize the city layouts and involve a geospatial relationship. In today's business environment, the AR technology paves the way for the return of investment largely in logistics, including transportation, warehouses, and route optimization. The warehouses workers wear smart AR glasses that provide the shortest path to pick the item from different places for shipping.

1.2 How Augmented Reality Works with Technology

1.2.1 Augmented Reality Functionality

The augmented reality functionality allows the user to control applications through real-world interactions, computers generate the output which is overlaid upon the real-world objects. On integrating AR functionality into the environment set of function blocks are grouped to sense the real-world objects, with the physical interactions, the AR functions observe the information about the physical world. It starts to capture the data of individual objects such as position, angle of rotation, camera distance. The output of the reality is mixed with physical objects as getting the input of the device camera and processed in the background which follows the position of the track and preserves the screen with the user interface.

By combining these simple interactions over the device sensors Augmented reality shows an overlaid layer on the physical object. These blocks are integrated with the AR functionalities for user interaction in real-world objects to the virtual cloud for ease, as shown in Figure 1.1.

1.2.1.1 Features of AR Technological Components

The technological components are found based on two systems one is server-side and the other is content provider where the virtual information is stored, this information can be projected on various devices like portable smartphones, head-mounted displays,

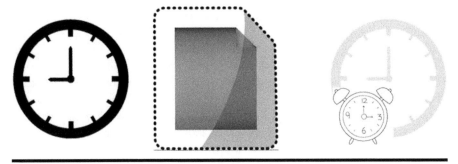

Figure 1.1 Printed, Black strip blocks on the clock, Overlaid timer upon the clock.

and glasses. A part of the content is made into small components and stored in various preferred machines the content provider server will act as a storage service that stores different data formats in the form of graphics, text, images, videos, and geographic information. It can be interactive with the device through protocol services to individual clients with various communication protocols like video protocol and network protocol. As in the part of the client-side, it works with the main component software framework, a part has units in which they require software in terms of firmware, an operating system that is supported by AR (Satyanarayanan, 2015).

The other component in the technology is the application browser to serve as detecting and tracking through recognition units uses camera API. The flow of technological components moves to the process of rendering that provides visualization which uses the computer graphical API and video components. The visualization is shown through the other important component User Interface that shows various gestures, voice, user interactions and gives the virtual touch feel of the objects with the technique called haptic. AR components feature connect in process of recognition unit which communicates through protocol services where the stored data from the content provider service taken to the other part of rendering process using graphics interface with this result the user feedback is been pushed to through the user interface and helps the user to feel the augmentation with the rendered visualization and virtual information produced from the devices for the physical environment.

1.2.1.2 The Methods to View Object with AR Feature Detection

Feature detection is needed to display virtual content or to place an object in some location in the real world first and foremost the device should detect that object and to put the character it is necessary to decide the proper area to place for that this feature detection is used. This technology is robust it means users move around without fixing at a location to view the virtual object in the real world so this technology is the speed in processing to give effective and accurate information. From the user's view if an object under a different position, a different angle the device will detect the same object in the same way for this feature detection is required (Drews, P., et.al., 2011). IPD is used for feature descriptors. The feature detection influences various factors like environment, changes in viewpoints, image scale, resolution, and lighting. A particular image is taken and using sample regions, interest point is detected and shown in circular or square regions, the scale determines the size of the regions in the image. This has different feature detection methods by considering the local image region gradients (Lowe, 2004), (Bay, Ess, Tuytelaars, & Van Gool, 2008, Juan et al., 2009). The other methods are identified using point-pair pixel intensity comparisons.

1.2.2 Feature Extraction Technologies Used in AR (Augmented Reality)

AR feature extraction starts with image acquisition, in such a way the interest points are detected and the feature extraction is done. To achieve feature extraction there is the various process to have proceeded with Grayscale Image Generation (GIG) – When AR device captures the image it is converted to a grayscale image for robustness, Integral Image Generation (IIG) – (Parmar & Desai, 2019). From grayscale image it is converted to an integral image this process of building it to enable the summation calculation over the sub-region images, Response Map Generation (RMG) – The image interest points are detected using the determinants of the image matrix to obtain this scale- space is required for that response map generation is used, Interest Point Detection (IPD) – On generating response map it can be accessed as interest point, Orientation Assignment (OA) – The detected IP provides image rotation by assigning it to the orientation process and Descriptor Detection (DD) – This descriptor identifies the IP uniquely and compares the descriptor with the data in the database and checks the qualification as invariability from noise, scale, rotation for this process descriptor detection is used. There are different kinds of descriptors available: Corner, Blob, and Region. Blob detection LoG (Laplacian of Gaussian), Hessian Matrix (H) second-order derivative, Laplacian trace of H is a process of detecting blobs in an image that has constant image properties all the points in a blob are considered to be similar to each other. These image properties that is brightness, color are used in the comparison process to surrounding regions. It also carries typical feature extraction techniques Haar feature (Messom & Barczak, 2009), HOG (Histogram of Oriented Gradient) (Jia & Zhang, 2009.

1.3 Hardare Components to Power Augmented Reality

1.3.1 The Hardware Needed to View AR Content

AR content is viewed with the help of various devices, some of them which include like Screens, glasses, handheld devices, mobile phones, head-mounted displays.

Table 1.2   Augmented Reality Hardware Devices

Augmented Reality Hardware	*Augmented Reality Devices*
Mobile Devices	
Holographic Displays	
Smart Glasses	
Immersed Head-Mounted Displays	

It involves technologies like SLAM (Simultaneous Localizing and Mapping) and Depth tracking that calculated the distance to the objects using sensors. The hardware components collect data with cameras and sensors to send data about the interaction of users for processing . It scans the surroundings and the device locates the physical objects to generate three-dimensional models to adapt the virtual layer with the detected physical environment. It can use a common smartphone to do the process and capture pictures or videos. This involves the technologies and detects the object (Thinkmobiles, 2017).

AR devices eventually should act like little computers, modern smartphones already do. In the same manner, they require a CPU, a GPS, flash memory, RAM, Bluetooth/Wi-Fi to be able to measure speed, angle, direction, orientation in space, and so on. The data collected from the sensor projects the digital content onto a surface or projects on AR headsets it shows the results of processing. Some AR devices assist the human eye to view the virtual images and mirrors are included to perform a proper image alignment (Thinkmobiles, 2017).

The core components required to power AR for developing applications and to set up the environment in AR can be divided into two different categories as software and hardware (Table 1.2).

1.3.2 *Hardware Requirements*

   a. Sensors
   b. A Camera
   c. Accelerometer

d. Gyroscope
e. Digital Compass
f. GPS (Sensing and tracking system), CPU
g. Display Screen, Smart Phones
h. A Network infrastructure
i. A Marker

1.3.3 Augmented Reality Devices

1.3.3.1 Software Requirements

a. A Content Service Provider
b. Web Services

An application or program running locally depends on various factors. The process of development has to assure placing additional reality to the end-user. To meet up this the hardware requirement and software requirements are needed to appear in the AR application to view and feel the augmentation. Technology helps that helps to define and detect the location to place the objects and includes all the hardware components to process. To present the augmented reality information software requirements involve giving the user 3D rendered model from rendering engine and animation gesture detection. Finally, the application program running locally presents the virtual content through the user interface to attain these software components that are used (Solutions, 2019). With these components, to provide augmentation experience there are tools available for environment and gadgets, this is covered with the common name called software development kit. The main feature of SDK gives visual information to the users with object interaction and supports any platform services it includes multi-target detection that is virtual buttons (Solutions, 2019).

1.3.3.2 AR Assets and ARCore Features

The hardware components find inside the smartphones or gadgets powers the augmented reality with the help of AR Assets that gives a real feel to the users. A digital asset is defined as an animated 3D model that binds with the real-world objects to experience the Augmented Reality which can also be benefitted in the business by demonstrating or advertising the product by allowing the customers to interact with the digital assets created like their products. Example: Items of furniture appear in the real environment which provides an option to decide to choose a better before the time of purchase. In this way, the creation of an asset is more important which provides interactiveness and engages the users with good satisfaction. It strives the user or consumers to use and interact with the digital representation. ARCore is a powerful tool for developers which gives a unique feature like cloud anchors which functions with cross-platform to experience in the different mobile operating system, Augmented faces functions with facial tracking by meshing 3D models without a depth sensor and environmental HDR focus on lighting extension from the real world onto virtual objects to make digital objects appear.

1.3.3.2.1 How the User Feels Real with Mobile Devices

To experience the real world and to give the user, the immersion in the objects which are not present in the real environment. Among the hardware requirements above mentioned it uses the assets to give the sense of realism and to start with the accelerometer the acceleration measures the change in velocity as to say mathematically speed divided by time, so the acceleration gives either static or dynamic that is motion or vibration state. Gyroscope works with the orientation feature it maintains in making the objects rotate and ensures the assets bind onto correctly. A camera gives the live feed of the real-world environment to overlay the virtual content and ARCore is more capable of using Google pixels which depends on machine learning, computer vision, and image processing to produce denser image quality for geolocation tagging. With this connection to enable the location-based augmented reality Magnetometer component of hardware is used and gives the direction where with this component it automatically knows which direction is north and it equates with the physical orientation to rotate the device. GPS receiver gets the time information from Global Navigation Satellite which provides geolocation here mobile devices act as a receiver, to enable location-based AR application uses ARCore.

1.3.3.2.2 AR Assets

The key point for AR creator is to focus on objects behavior when embedding the real environment and virtual layer simultaneously here placing the assets and positioning to one point when the devices or users are in motion is more important to makes stay the object where it is already to be positioned this kind is known as placing the assets. Next, it should be able to scale and size which has to incorporate with a placed object.

If there are more than one virtual content or object in the same environment, devices overlay both the content one above the other so it breaks the sense of immersion to the user to avoid this kind, a technique called occlusion is used where it makes understand the hardware about the presence of objects and the relative distance of it. In this way, the technique hides the unwanted object and views the required content to give the real feel with the AR application. With this alone the real experience cannot be given, the virtual object response is required according to the pattern for this color, shadows, and lightning is essential if the object is moved and shadow needs to move accordingly as happens in real-life for these effect shadow assets are used. The other important asset is solid augmented where the AR creator must be aware that virtual objects should not overlay on the real-world objects, for this solid augmented asset is used and context awareness on digital object fidelity, smoothness, and functionality. The context-awareness needs to be maintained by both hardware and software by tracking the anchored virtual object present in the environment and understanding its size and shape individually.

1.3.3.2.3 ARCore

ARCore achieves optimal realism using both the hardware and software parts of AR. The environmental information is scanned, recognized, segmented, and analyzed, these processes are involved for tracking. ARCore mainly does motion-tracking this uses the SLAM technology. This process collects the hardware data information to create an environment understanding for rendering augmentation by detecting the feature points to set appropriate anchors. The process used in AR is known as COM (Concurrent Odometry and Mapping), it tells the smartphone about the located space in the environment this is called feature points. The awareness is created with inertia data of feature points and also the smartphone movement information using ARCore. The smartphone position can be de-termined with the use of a gyroscope which gives the present angle of the device and the accelerometer gives the speed of the phone now ARCore determines the position of the phone and finds the assets to be placed. To detect the flat surface ARCore software uses the hardware component information together of gyroscope and accelerometer to create context-awareness. The environment light is estimated by scanning the image pixels which determines the average incoming light that helps to decide and set the incoming light which is used by ARCore. The ARCore makes the user feel real by providing the shadows and lighting by matching it to the environment in games. If the motion tracking fails or drifts, when the device position is not reflected with the actual environment anchors can be used by setting it up with the static digital object or plane. In a specific location if the anchor is placed when the user places the device it holds the object accurately and detects the feature points to provide the virtual object in the static position to stay visible and placed consistently in the environment. Likewise, ARCore software uses a cluster of filter points to appear on the surface to determine the boundary of the plane and make the information to be viewed in the AR application. To rest the virtual information on a flat surface, the same information produced by ARCore from the boundary can also be used (Cammeron, 2018).

1.3.4 Real-World Uses of Augmented Reality

The AR applications work on the live feed of the camera into the digital content which is likely embedded into the use of real-world scenarios. Some of the ex-amples are the entertainment and gaming field making good use of AR. As an example, the famous AR game Pokemon GO. With the use of augmented reality hardware devices, many medical students are trained with the technology wearing the AR headsets to practice medical training and integrates with various platforms to perform invasive surgeries.

Mechanical Engineers: The methods of AR help the engineers to learn the service and maintenance in real-time with the AR glasses and learns the live guides, getting an idea of improving the efficacy of technical machine repairs and speed up services for customers. These are some of the real-world use cases with AR technologies.

1.3.5 The Advantages of Various AR UI (User Interface) Types

1. AR application gives real-world training to make it easier and process new concepts for students, this makes improvisation of education in clarity learning and helps to acquire skills with capabilities.
2. Visualizing 3D objects created by merging the virtual objects with the real world helps to provide digital information and detailed insights.
3. AR offers guidance to enhance customer services. For example, AR glasses used by sales professionals to help customers to buy cosmetics enhance the aesthetics.
4. AR headsets play a major role by adding a video of the car as a virtual layer into the existing environment to evaluate and estimate the cost of the damaged car to fix it. This kind helps the insurance worker to process the claims precisely and it changes the way of business operations easier.
5. The advantage of using Augmented Reality application is that gives additional information about the surroundings of the product present in the real-time which makes user retrieve valuable information with its characteristics.
6. The user also gets benefited from a unique function that adds up value for the buying process on creating interaction with consumers on a merchant site.
7. AR creates a drive-in business growth and many AR application have emerged to reach the audience with new services as software industries turn towards AR application development to exchange information and explore the technological advancements for business developments.
8. The significant benefit is visualizing and thinking in a three-dimensional view so it made a revolution in the field of advertising and marketing.

The transformation takes place in the real world with the incredible features of AR when it is demonstrated to assist, entertain, and educate people.

1.4 Augmented Reality Business Applications

Augmented reality has made a huge impact on creating business values in broader ways which help organizations around the globe to become a product of themselves and improve the performance across the value chain. There are various business areas where the augmented technology paves the way to shape business activities to digitize the products on rebuilding and improvising the existing products.

1.4.1 AR Today: Smart Phone vs. Standalone

In today's world, AR is made possible with smartphones which act as a portal giving information and experience to the new world. The rapid growth of the AR industry is mainly because of the contribution from the side of mobile devices, all the features which are required for an AR application are needed for mobile as hardware components: gyroscope, accelerometer, high-resolution displays. The smartphone itself creates AR with front and rear-facing cameras, with this integrated information and the digital objects, are displayed in mobile devices.

1.4.2 AR for Weather Prediction

Weather forecasting to give graphics, digital effects to forecast the weather information is challenging for the forecaster. The basic element previously used were setting Chroma key projecting blue or green screen behind with a graphic feed from a computer. The technology effectively helps the forecaster to interact with the graphics and to broadcast visual interests this seems to be an AR-type presentation for forecasting the weather. Augmented Reality for weather forecasting is because it gives visualization in a four-dimensional view and adds inherent value for the forecaster ease to hold the attention of the audience through live interaction with dynamic 3D images of storms and atmospheric events. It is also useful in enabling travel conditions information to the audience by integrating traffic data into an on-air presentation that assists to provide real visual content. The advanced AR technology is used for displaying live radar, storm timing feature, rainfall totals, and flooding impact in a virtual set, many companies work on this part using the technology for weather prediction through this it helps the captivate viewers to hold their attention.

1.4.3 AR for Market Prediction

Augmented reality contributes to gaming, sports, entertainment, and education, as it is the base of strong consumers the market prediction technology, predicts the growth of the Augmented Reality market by finding information about a product, real-time stock, and sales information. Finally resulted that the vast majority of growth is been raised and reaches 85 percent in global market size.

The main key growth is in the area of health, manufacturing, and retail sectors it is been derived from the compound annual growth rate.

1.4.3.1 AR for Business Models

Augmented Reality is so effective in the business models on developing various models in different domains like architecture which is benefitted by the archaeological information and gives plans for the rebuilding of ruins, arts and performance provides some useful assistance on using the technology by giving musical notes and services for sound coordination's. In terms of Education, students are given customized assistance for complex subjects by interactive computer simulation of concepts to experience and explore them (Kurubacak, G., Altinpulluk, H., n.d., 2017). In Medical Science and Engineering, it guides the doctors and nurses to follow the procedure and support in the right way by providing services like health scan of patients and robotic surgery support, then this technology also used by military defense operations and serves as assistance for providing situational awareness.

The techniques using Augmented Reality to identify the movement of each player in sports and entertainment. It enables the commercial value for every domain by the advertisements overlaid in real-time onto the user's view. Navigational information and guidance of historical events are displayed so it is used in tourism and sightseeing likewise the same information can also be displayed on automobile windshields to prevent accidents by giving specific attention to the drivers. The domain of AR provides platforms with toolboxes and custom services for application development also industry-specific developments and self-services it tests with content management tools.

1.4.3.2 Market Analysis of the AR Market (Market Size Forecast)

The forecast of market share for AR, focusing on a head-mounted display and all other components grow significantly in the future. The major type of services in the market for Augmented Reality devices are video games, video entertainment, and health care in all other applications it has a rapid growth. The forecast of the market size in 2025 says slow improvisation in user experiences in technology usage, seamlessly mobility supports a lot with the display, safety, and privacy. The head-mounted display is more popular and the system behaves and operates sufficiently well. Extensible mobility evolves the market size of AR in 2025 to become a generic computing platform.

1.4.4 AR for Smart Cities

The technology overlays digital content in the real world. As the emergence of AR engines like ARCore and many other usage and access to technology is been increased in the market. Due to the extensive availability of network connectivity and smart devices around the environment surrounding augmented reality plays a major role in powering its feature into smart cities. Some of the features like navigation services, live tracking, intelligent road work assistance, and much more make AR explored in all the domains as it provides public services on managing and controlling street lights, parking, etc. in a single platform. AR can be experienced with simulating the city services and collecting the data readings from the smart devices and environmental sensors which are embedded into the mobile devices to provide data based on location.

1.5 Tools Available for Augmented Reality and Recognition

Augmented Reality has many tools available to create digitally enhanced features for warfare emergent programs that prevails from serious conditions. The possibilities of AR technology are limitless on integrating the tools into devices. Various software tools can incorporate into the applications to create AR-based featured applications.

1.5.1 Software Tools: AR with Tools like Google Poly and Unity

■ **Poly**

An online library is used by the people to browse and remix the 3D assets or 3D models, the asset can be created by any model developing platforms or tools like a block that generates a file it can be uploaded into the poly library and direct object file also can be uploaded. It is an Application Programming Interface (API), with this it contains thousands of assets and it can be accessed freely for the developers to browse, search, view, and add create applications.

■ **Software Development Kit (SDK)**

AR application can be developed in Java using high-level 3D frameworks it offers a library for android it will integrate for AR experience which combines with ARCore API for rendering, plugins can be used to import and preview the assets directly in Android Studio.

■ **Creation of Sceneform**

Scene form is a plugin used for developing three-dimensional applications without working with complex APIs like OpenGL. To create Sceneform using Android Studio adds the plugin from preferences:

Android Studio > Preferences > Plugins > Browse Repositories > Google Sceneform tools (Beta)

After adding the plugin automatically all the assets are imported and the source file is created into the project, this contains three supported files they are

1. The object file (obj) – It is a file format that contains three-dimensional coordination of an object.
2. Filmbox file (fbX) – It is used as interoperability for creating digital content.
3. GL Transmission Format (glTF) – It stores information about 3D models in JSON format.

Now Sceneform will convert the source file into a.sfb format that is runtime optimized format and this will be added to the.apk file. Right-click on the model imported and an import wizard dialog box opens just click the finish button the asset will be imported. The plugin will add the imported asset to the Gradle file to create a new runtime optimized format. By this render views the asset through sfb file viewer without deploying into the mobile it shows like WYSIWYG (What You See Is What You Get) on the phone screen. Using Sceneform SDK an android AR application is been created.

▪ Unity

A popular cross-platform game engine has a great visual interface for creating both 3D and 2D objects and interactive applications, video games, AR contents, Films, and many other projects. It contains many tools to create objects and environments. Unity can be used with ARCore and can import the objects from poly to incorporate into the developing applications this gives the unique experience exclusively unity platform is used to create AR content. The toolkit is used in unity and import assets at edit time and run time. To run on mobile devices it relies on ARCore and ARKit.

1.5.1.1 AR Technological Software Approaches

Augmented Reality can be carried out with the main technology called Simultaneous Localizing and Mapping. This technology is used significantly in AR applications and it is applicable for no prior reference points. In SLAM, as the machine or device to understand the visual content collected data from a sensor that is recognized as a reference point, it helps the machine to differentiate between the objects around the surrounding like roads, walls, and floors. But with this technology, the SLAM does not require any prior reference points instead it has the capability of localizing the virtual object without any prior map or GPS signal it navigates through space (Mayekar, 2018). SLAM uses some algorithms to map the objects that simultaneously localize to find the location of physical objects and fits with the preexisting device layout and framework of the environment. It is done possibly only with the mathematical and statistical algorithms where SLAM largely makes use.

In the initial state, the measurement leads to uncertainty and it is solved with the method by factoring in noise. Among all the algorithms this technology exclusively uses the Kalman filter to predict the position and find the unknown variables of 3D objects whereas the same algorithm is also used by Google for its self-driving cars. It is an autonomous technology that creates the map of its surroundings, augmentation is done with the existing Google maps upon these algorithms come into the play to find the different probabilities of outcomes.

Many AR software tool developers use a probabilistic approach to give the system accurately measured decisions. As the same, this technology simply localizes data from sensors for their environment, at the same time the structure of the environment also gets mapped. It mainly aims to solve the mapping problem as now all the software development kit for AR provides upon this technology functionalities (NewGenApps, 2020). Marker-based AR in other ways maker is termed as recognition this identifies the objects, based on natural feature tracking. The marker is sensed with the use of a mobile device by that the augmented reality and overlays the virtual or digital information in the physical environment this kind also makes sense in the part of AR technology.

1.5.2 Types of Recognition

1. Markerless (Jin D., et.al., 2011)
2. Marker-based
3. Projection-based
4. Superimposition – based

1.5.2.1 Native Software Solutions – ARKit and ARCore (Recognizing the Ground Plane)

The difference in ARKit and ARCore both are frameworks but differ in the operating system. ARKit works only in android and the other framework supports iOS devices. As all the framework does its advancement is with motion tracking and allows the device to understand the links with the real-world environment. ARCore mainly helps to detect the position of the phone with the gyroscope component available in all smartphones. This ARCore is used by all the google pixel mobiles, Oneplus, Samsung, Huawei, Asus, and Zenfone, it is compatible with these brand handsets as default features like AR stickers in the camera application. The same is for ARKit but it is limited to iOS devices (Cammeron, 2018).

Common Feature for both ARKit and ARCore:

1. Motion Tracking
2. Plane Detection
3. Lighting Estimation

■ **Motion Tracking**

The basic requirement for AR must have a mobile device with the functionality of detecting the device's position and its orientation. It is made with a feature called Virtual Inertial Odometry (VIO). The spatial data movement is detected by collecting the data from the motion sensor and the environment. The smartphone device understands and tracks the location with the relative position of the realistic environment. The Augmented Reality platform with its common features environment is detected with the location of the flat horizontal surfaces, size, current lighting conditions, and topology, and user expression in the face.

■ Plane Detection

ARCore understands the environment to place the object by plane detection. In other cases, the ARKit takes as the scene detection for semantic linking of the environment with the device. There is a difference between the two software development kits. This feature is called depth perception it detects the tables, floors, and all the flat surfaces where the limitations of the framework cannot measure the vertical planes because sensors in smartphones are limited for AR capabilities.

■ Lighting Estimation

Dynamic lighting effects are placed in the scene which applies the effect of ambient light sensed by the camera where photorealistic rendering of virtual objects is applied (Shavel, 2019). It is a feature of light metering, which allows the smartphone to detect the position of the environment with the presence of current lighting effects.

1.5.2.2 Vuforia Animation Markers

Vuforia is software to develop AR applications and it is a client-side library. It is supported by all the Vuforia engine-supported platforms. This engine includes the C hash language for Unity and Java for android. This uses the cross-platform game engines to build applications: Android Studio, Visual Studio/Unity, Xcode (Vuforia, 2018). Viewing the Animated Character model using Unity3D and Vuforia, the steps to view before login into the Vuforia develop portal proceed to the develop tab and choose the target manager to create a database with the device type. After creating the database add a target on selecting an image and setting its width. Now the target is created and the active target will be downloaded select a development platform as Unity editor after compiling a traceable database it finalizes and saves the downloaded file into the machine. In downloads of Vuforia SDK 4.2 version shows:

1. SDK for Android
2. SDK for iOS
3. Unity Extension

Among the above-listed choose Unity extension and add the license key by entering the application name as already created before, open Unity application and create a new project

a. Delete the default main camera and lights.
b. Select Import custom package from assets and choose the Vuforia unity extension file downloaded.
c. Select Import custom package from assets and choose the Vuforia project created with a database.
d. Drag and drop the ARCamera and Image Target in the asset of Unity.
e. Copy the license key of the Vuforia project and paste it in the QCAR Behavior script which is available in the inspector of the unity platform and check the data set option from the menu.
f. Now select the Image Target option and select the Vuforia project
g. Place the animated 3D model above the target image plane and modify the scale values
h. Add video and audio source to the 3D model and run the file. Now AR object created in Unity interacts with the real-time environment

1.5.2.2.1 Main Feature

a. **Object Targets**

It has categories of features in Vuforia Images, Objects, and Environment. Images feature includes Image target, Multi-Target, Cylinder Targets. Objects include Object Reco, VuMark, Model targets. The environment includes Area targets, Device tracking, Ground plane, Vuforia fusion.

1.5.2.2.2 Tools

Vuforia collective has six different tools to create targets, store the targets in the database, and used them as a secured application. To use these tools and develop any AR apps requires a license key to work. It can be generated by the license manager which is associated with the service plans. After unlocking the tools with the license key, it is free to access the tools for creating desktop applications that create targets for 3D scanned images of an environment. The developed application can be pre-compiled as code once and deploy on mobile devices any number of times, it looks like a.apk file to test the area target application. The target is created from pre-existing 3D objects using the Vuforia tool model target generator. It supports specific formats like:.obj,.fbx,.vrml,.igs,.pvg,.stl,.dae,.stp. With this format, an object scanner the Vuforia can scan the 3D objects easily with the engine.

1.5.2.2.3 Target Manager and Cloud Service

For developing a web application target manager is used to create database and cloud services to store the targets. Vuforia provides cloud recognition services to store a large number of targets and images to fetch during the scan of 3D objects. The image storing database is supported by Vuforia web service API which enables integration with the content management provider. As it is a client-side library the application programming interface bridges the gap to provide the digital contents stored for the created targets.

1.5.2.3 Recognition of Codes with Subsequent Placement – Zappar

The name Zappar itself explains as it is an AR application which adds a new feature of making the phone camera reimagine by connecting to the remote control when the zap app is connected that views graphics, images, text, mail actions, videos, motion controls, transitions, and many features are added up to give new dimension on turning any printed hard copies into an interactive channel for the users which gives delightful experience. The application is open-source used in both iOS and Android.

Zappar creates an illusion and multimedia interaction which can be used for e-learning and education to make the children understand complex subjects by using the application creating graphical transitions and collection of multimedia to explain the subject upon the printed materials or books available in hand this integrates with the workplace to make real the learning experience better to create more interest on the subject and gives conceptual view.

This means that subject books or notebooks or any subject printed materials can have AR icons where the students and teachers can interact with a classroom or in any environment on their mobile devices and gadgets. Zappar has already two products to meet the challenge:

  a. Zapcode Creator
  b. Zappar Studio

1.5.2.3.1 Creating a Zapcode with Zappar

Zapcode is a web-based application it works the same as the QR code, the main difference varies mainly in reading the content. Zapcode is generated and printed in the handouts for the mobile devices to scan through the application to view the interactive elements.

Step 1. In the Zappar pro editor environment download the image for Zapcode in SVG format.
Step 2. Upload the tracking image or the front page of the book, flyer, and posters or as an Advertisement
Step 3. Place images, graphical contents, videos, transitions, actions, and services.
Step 4. Place the Zapcode on the image before uploading it. Download the Zapcode graphic add it to the tracking image.

Zapcode for Bharathiar University

Figure 1.2   Zapcode for Viewing Bharathiar University Logo.

Step 5. Set up with the Properties, Actions, Transitions, and Appearance as required.

Step 6. Modify the properties of the scene and save it.

Step 7. Publish and preview it with the Zapcode application as shown in Figure 1.2 (Alexander. 2016).

Figure 1.2 shows the of Zapcode before and after aiming at the tracking image seen in the colorless mode from the created project and with published content. The basic project created with the workspace on ZapWorks Designer, which is a platform that helps to create an Augmented Reality experience by creating simple Zapcode with drag and drop tools available. Figure 1.2 shows two different images one is a Zapcode that is placed without a tracking image, briefly to say about the tracking image it does not have any background picture. On the other side of the figure is with the Bharathiar University Logo attached above the first image it views after scanning the Zapcode with a smartphone camera automatically detects and displays the created content with transitions and objects added. As to the above figure it after scanning the Zapcode it displays the logo of the university and direct links to the website and shows the transition effects with an image. This kind helps to experience the technology Augmented Reality in real-time.

1.5.2.3.2 Products Available under ZapWorks

The products in ZapWorks manages in three different views like create, publish, track, and manage. Under create it shows on ZapWork studio and other is ZapWork designer, in publish view shows Zappar applications, Web AR, Custom applications. Track and manage shows Zap analytics as shown in Table 1.3.

1.5.2.4 Location-Based Tracking – Wikitude

Wikitude supports 12 different varieties of development frameworks which created powerful AR applications that blend the digital and physical world with the Wikitude

Table 1.3   Products and Features of ZapWorks.

Create	ZapWorks Studio	Feature-rich tool
	ZapWorks Designer	Drag and Drop tool
Publish	Web AR	Browser access
	Custom App Solutions	Explore AR features
	Zappar App	Instant preview
Track and Manage	Zap analytics	Analytics Dashboard

SDK. It is supported by cross-platform and supports many features like scene recognition, Instant targets, Unity live preview, extended object tracking, support for windows UWP, and many more. The AR applications with Wikitude can be developed in any framework with choices like JavaScript, Unity, Cordova, Xamarin, Flutter, React Native, ARCore, ARKit, Ionic, Adobe Air, LBAR, Qt by Felgo.

1.5.2.4.1 Wikitude Software Development Kit

The software development kit for a mobile application to experience Augmented Reality in any kind of location with the location tracking technology and android applications can be created with AR feature by building upon Wikitude SDK using different components shown in Table 1.4.

The components in Wikitude SDK Android have a computed engine that includes four different optimizations of graphical processors, core components come under an application programming interface with calibration manager, plugin manager, GeoAR, and Cloud Recognition. Here the main part is recognized with the plugin interface which is used by all platforms because it owns various recognition APIs, SLAM engine, ARCore, and ARKit. The native APIs give direct access to the Wikitude computer engine for android, iOS, and Windows on top of the native APIs Unity plugin allows Wikitude SDK to access with the combination of the plugin.

Table 1.4   Components of Software Development Kit – Wikitude

WebView	
Plugin (Unity)	
Sensor Manager	Render Manager
Components	APIs
Compute Engine	

The powerful features available here are (ARPost, 2018)

1. Tracking the location of the user
2. Even when the camera focus is away the Interaction takes place.
3. Compatibility support by resuming on different devices to recreate the AR application.
4. Unity engines give increased stability and performance by live preview
5. Supported by Windows platform

1.5.2.4.2 Tracking the Location of the User

This feature is possible with scene recognition to allow the system to understand the real world where the user is located. When the scene is recognized the user location is tracked with the use of GPS which enables the placement of realistic objects the real interaction between the graphical object and user takes place.

1.5.2.4.3 Object Tracking

When the user moves away from the trigger marker, this feature works with the extended object tracking method, its advantage is that it saves and shares the virtual content and navigates the user to the trigger maker automatically.

1.5.2.4.4 Instant Targets

AR application development can be shared with friends and it can be resumed in other devices to recreate it, the main feature is marking the specific point and marking it as instant targets where it is saved and can also be recorded as a video. This kind helps in industrial equipment or machine if any flaws occur the instant targets can be created and shared with the expert to rectify it an immediately main advantage in it is saving.

1.5.2.4.5 Unity Live Preview

This new feature helps the developer to select the live preview with a remote camera that the smartphone act as a control, the projection of the developing object will be easily previewed before deploying it and the perspective of the developer will be clear in the test period. The image tracking in the editor using Unity remote application as shown in Figure. 1.3

1.6 Conclusion

Augmented reality a set of technologies that have changed the face of mobile applications which seeks the digital to integrate with the real world. The several flavors of AR

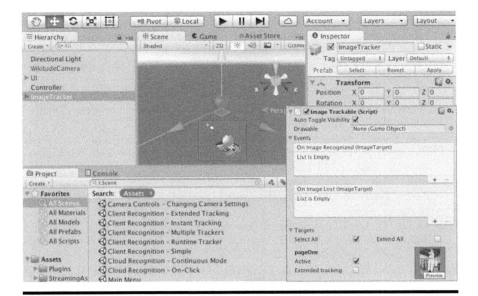

Figure 1.3   Unity Live Preview with Unity Remote Application.

help the users to perceive both reality and digitally supplied information through the tools and applications. The study on designing AR applications to adapt technology in response to challenges and compares the features of technologies. Applications and current use in augmented reality in all sorts of places and industries are discussed in brief. The challenges and real-time scenarios of AR technologies with various hardware and software-based technological approaches are focused in-depth and explained.

References

Alexander, S. (2016). Augmented Reality: From Concept To Execution - Elearning Industry. eLearning Industry, https://elearningindustry.com/augmented-reality-concept-execution. [Accessed 6 April 2020].

ARPost (2018). Wikitude 8, The SDK For Shared Augmented Reality Experiences, rpost. co https://arpost.co/2018/06/08/wikitude-8-sdk-shared-augmented-reality-experiences. [Accessed 7 March 2020].

Azuma, R. (1997). A Survey of Augmented Reality. *Presence: Teleoperators and Virtual Environments*, 6(4), 355–385. doi: 10.1162/pres.1997.6.4.355.

Bay, H., Ess, A., Tuytelaars, T., & Van Gool, L. (2008). Speeded-Up Robust Features (SURF). *Computer Vision and Image Understanding*, 110(3), 346–359. doi: 10.1016/j.cviu.2007.09.01.

Bederson, B. (1995). Audio Augmented Reality: A Prototype Automated Tour Guide. In: Conference on Human Factors in Computing Systems. Denver, Colorado, USA: Mosaic of Creativity: CHI '95 Conference Proceedings, pp. 1–2.

Cammeron, S. (2018). What Are The Arcore And Arkit Augmented Reality Frameworks? How-To Geek, https://www.howtogeek.com/348445/what-are-the-arcore-and-arkit-augmented-reality-frameworks/. [Accessed 10 March 2020].

Craig, A. (2013). *Understanding Augmented Reality* 1st edn,. Amsterdam: Elsevier Publishers, 296 pp.

Drews, P., de Bem, R., & de Melo, A. (2011). Analyzing and exploring feature detectors in images. In: 9th IEEE International Conference on Industrial Informatics (INDIN). Lisbon, Portugal: IEEE, pp. 305–310.

Financesonline.com (2020). 45 Vital Augmented Reality Statistics: 2020 Market Share & Data Analysis - Financesonline.Com., https://financesonline.com/augmented-reality-statistics/. [Accessed 12 March 2020].

Geospatial (2018). Difference between Augmented Reality, Virtual Reality, and Mixed Reality. YouTube. URL https://www.youtube.com/watch?v=3mr_S5mOtsw [Accessed 13 August 2018].

Hubspot (2018). What is the difference between Augmented Reality (AR) and Virtual Reality (VR)?. YouTube. URL https://www.youtube.com/watch?v=ZQ2XO7HerfI [Accessed 30 August 2018].

Jia, H., & Zhang, Y. (2009). Multiple Kernels Based Object Tracking Using Histograms of Oriented Gradients. *Acta Automatica Sinica*, *35*(10), 1283–1289. doi: 10.3724/sp.j.1 004.2009.01283

Jin, D., Um, K., & Cho K. (2011). Development of Real-Time Markerless Augmented Reality System Using Multi-thread Design Patterns. In: T. Kimet al. (eds), *Multimedia, Computer Graphics, and Broadcasting. MulGraB 2011. Communications in Computer and Information Science*, vol 262, (pp. 155–164). Berlin, Heidelberg: Springer

Juan, L., & Gwun, O. (2009). A comparison of SIFT, PCA-SIFT, and SURF., *International Journal of Image Processing*, *3*(4), 143–152.

K. J., Parmar, & Desai, A. (2019). Feature Extraction in Augmented Reality, cs.GR, arXiv: 1911.09177v1.

Kipper, G., & Rampolla, J. (2013). *Augmented Reality*. 1st edn. Syngress, Waltham: Elsevier Publishers, Mass., pp. 208

Kurubacak, G., & Altinpulluk, H., n.d. (2017). Mobile Technologies And Augmented Reality In Open Education. *IGI Global*, Turkey, pp. 300.

Lowe, D. (2004). Distinctive Image Features from Scale-Invariant Keypoints. *International Journal of Computer Vision*, *60*(2), 91–110. doi: 10.1023/B:VISI.0000029664.99615.94.

Mayekar, S. (2018). The Future Of AR Is SLAM Technology. But What Is SLAM?, Analytics Insight. Analytics Insight. https://www.analyticsinsight.net/future-ar-slam-technology-slam/. [Accessed 15 April 2020].

Messom, C., & Barczak, A. (2009). Stream processing for fast and efficient rotated Haar-like features using rotated integral images. *International Journal of Intelligent Systems Technologies and Applications*, *7*(1), 40. doi: 10.1504/ijista.2009.025105.

Mordorintelligence.co. (2020). Augmented Analytics Market Size, Trends, Forecast (2020–2025). https://www.mordorintelligence.com/industry-reports/augmented-analytics-market. [Accessed (10 April 2020)].

NewGenApps (2020). The technology company with integrity. Know The Augmented Reality Technology: How Does AR Work? - Newgenapps The Technology Company With Integrity. https://www.newgenapps.com/blog/augmented-reality-technology-how-ar-works. [Accessed 18 April 2020].

Olsson, T., & Salo, M. (2011). Online user survey on current mobile augmented reality applications. 2011 10th IEEE International Symposium on Mixed and Augmented Reality, 75–84. doi: 10.1109/ISMAR.2011.6092372.

PRNewswire. (2020). The Global Augmented Reality Software Market Is Expected To Grow From USD 4,123.12 Million In 2018 To USD 16,489.12 Million By The End Of 2025 A Compound Annual Growth Rate (CAGR) Of 21.89%. Prnewswire.com, https://www.prnewswire.com/news-releases/the-global-augmented-reality-software-market-is-expected-to-grow-from-usd-4-123-12-million-in-2018-to-usd-16-489-12-million-by-the-end-of-2025-at-a-compound-annual-growth-rate-cagr-of-21-89-301029592.html. [Accessed 12 February 2020].

Satyanarayanan, M. (2015). A Brief History of Cloud Offload. *GetMobile: Mobile Computing and Communications, 18*(4), 19–23. doi: 10.1145/2721914.2721921.

Shavel, T. (2019). Arcore Vs. Arkit: Which Is Better For Building Augmented Reality Apps?.Iflexion, https://www.iflexion.com/blog/arcore-vs-arkit. [Accessed 9 April 2020].

Solutions, T. (2019). Advantages Of Using Augmented Reality For Business. Theappsolutions.com. https://theappsolutions.com/blog/development/ar-benefits-for-business. [Accessed 13 May 2019].

Tech Jury (2019). 20 Augmented Reality Stats To Keep You Sharp In 2020 - Tech Jury.net https://techjury.net/augmented-reality/#gref. [Accessed 14 March 2020].

Thinkmobiles (2017). What Is Augmented Reality (AR) And How Does It Work. https://thinkmobiles.com/blog/what-is-augmented-reality. [Accessed 14December2018].

Vuforia (2018). Overview, Library.vuforia.com, https://library.vuforia.com/getting-started/overview.html. [Accessed 12 April 2020].

Chapter 2

Industry 4.0: Augmented and Virtual Reality in Education

P. Bhanu Prasad[1], N. Padmaja[2], B. Satish Kumar[3], and A. Aravind[4]

[1]Research Mentor, Sree VidyanikethanEngg College, Tirupati, India & Chief Mentor, Sahajanand Laser Technology Ltd, India
[2]Professor, Department of ECE, Centre for Communications and Signal Processing, Sree Vidyanikethan Engineering College, Tirupati, India
[3]B.Tech, Department of ECE, Sree Vidyanikethan Engineering College, Tirupati, India
[4]B.Tech, Department of Mechanical Engineering, Sree Vidyanikethan Engineering College, Tirupati, India

Contents

DOI: 10.1201/9781003175896-2

29

2.1 Introduction

Augmented reality (AR) and virtual reality (VR) technology has begun to penetrate the education system deeply. Students, learners, teachers, and trainers have started to exploit this technology in several ways as the technology has advanced, including user-generated internet, mobile phones, and wearables. The students are exposed to new ways of accessing information in the open world with access to teachers, and they also have opportunities to collaborate with other learners.

Education 5.0 based learning is no longer centered on the interaction between teachers and student learners. Students are often involved in their approach to networking either directly or indirectly with diverse information sources through a manipulated interactive open world. This process of Education 5.0 stimulated the development of a more sophisticated, tailored process of learning that enables the student's individuality, growth, learning pace, and exceptional attitude of learning to be celebrated. Education 5.0 is a desired and promising approach to learning and understanding that aligns with the evolving fourth industrial revolution (and also is flexible to adapt to Industry 5.0) and can adjust to the individual learner's pace and interest using artificial intelligence, robotic process automation, along with extended reality (XR).

Education 5.0 is about developing and evolving new technologies parallel with recent trends. Especially in higher education institutions, this means understanding the future requirements of the graduates to be successful in the industry. As far as universities are concerned, they must follow various strategies and prepare the pupils for a world where technology is changing fast across all industries. This means that the curriculum and approach to learning altogether need to be dynamically adapted by improving the university experience through practical knowledge with a deeper blend of technology into the teaching and learning process. Education 5.0 embraces the advanced analytics and techniques that involve treating each pupil as an individual, thereby understanding everybody's learning desires and outcomes. The Education 5.0 process adapts to each student to achieve five Cs: Communication, collaboration, competence, creativity, and critical thinking. This is only possible using XR, where the virtual labs can dynamically be changed in such a way that the practical experiments will be aligned to the needs of the industry. By aligning teaching and learning methods (shifting the focus from teaching to learning), universities can be sure about the preparedness of their graduates to be successful in the future.

Since the digital era, a huge amount of data have been collected from several sources. For better decision making, it is important to collect the right information at the right time and to showcase them in the right context. The Industry 4.0 revolution depends on nine pillars to achieve this. Among these technologies, one of the important foundation pillars is AR, VR, and mixed reality (MR). The common term XR is associated with any AR, VR, or MR (X stands for A, V, or M). XR is an essential component of Education 5.0 to understand that everybody's learning requirements and interests as well as outcomes are unique and adapt the learning process to bridge the gap between industry needs and academic learning (Liu, Dede, Huang, & Richards, 2017).

XR recognizes the group of technologies that enable viewing real-world situations in an augmented way by overlapping computer-generated graphics in the form of text, images, audio, and video with interaction in the virtual world together with the real world. This pictorial facet in the physical environment is improved by adopting the use of numerous devices. XR has diverse applications in the manufacturing domain, which has been the most attractive world of XR until now. With the advent of the Industry 4.0 revolution in education, XR has taken a step ahead to convert book-based education to an interactive and more interesting way of learning.

There is a gap between academics and industry due to the static knowledge taught at academic organizations. This is due to rapid changes in industries to use emerging technologies and the time taken by academic organizations to modify and adapt their curricula. Concerned with various processes to transform academic curricula to industrial needs by adding value to the components, XR surely can remain a game changer. This is because real-time data are needed at several phases of the education life cycle. Books may have theoretical foundations, and they can be visualized as industrial applications by augmenting the necessary information from books, materials, etc., using XR. Thus, XR can be a real boon in these complex progressions since it is proficient to assist, simulate, and thereby improve the processes even before they are carried out.

As industry has already started using XR for manufacturing in all stages from design aspects to prototype modeling, from production and assembly to maintenance, every single stage has its own sets of encounters that are overcome by the simulation of the process and procedures to diminish the downtime and rationalize the operations by using XR. It is now time for academic organizations to be open to this idea of utilizing XR and reducing the gap between academia and industry. This chapter explains the basic concepts of XR along with examples of how XR can be better utilized in education. Figure 2.1 shows the process of evolving from reality to virtual reality. Figure 2.2 depicts the difference between VR, AR and MR.

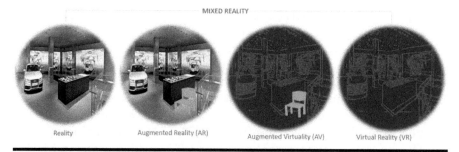

Figure 2.1 Reality to Virtual Reality.

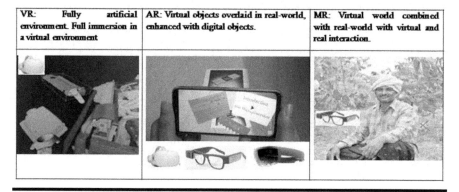

VR: Fully artificial environment. Full immersion in a virtual environment	AR: Virtual objects overlaid in real-world, enhanced with digital objects.	MR: Virtual world combined with real-world with virtual and real interaction.

Figure 2.2 Difference between VR, AR, and MR.

2.2 Augmented Reality

AR augments our real and practical world by including layers of digital data in the real world. The augmented world appears in a straight view of the prevailing environment and adds multi-dimensional traces of sounds, videos, and graphics into it. Three-dimensional (3D) models are virtually projected on top of the physical things in real time. Augmentation happens in real-time scenarios and within the framework of the environment. AR is the view of the actual real-time scenarios that are overlaid by simulated images with the description that enables changing the insight of reality. The AR applications influence our social life habits, learning, purchasing, marketing, and the entertainment industry. AR applications classically link digitally simulated animations onto a distinct "marker", or with the aid of sensors in mobile devices locate the location, and identify the needed information to augment.

AR helps users to understand real objects better by overlapping information. This makes the learning process much easier and more interesting. Users can judge and buy the products that suit their needs; they can visualize environments they cannot see (blind people, military) and better organize classrooms (automatic attendance, identify the student and respond).

The term "augmented reality" was coined in 1990 and was used in television, in the film industry, and by the military. With the rise of fast internet, smartphones, smart glasses, haptics, and sensors, AR is rapidly growing in every part of our life, like education, training, marketing, remote maintenance, shopping, military, real estate, games, and sports. With the growth of future technology, AR has potential uses and will become part of our everyday life.

The process of AR includes capturing a 3D image of the real world, detection and tracking of objects of interest in the image, overlapping the computer-generated information in 3D on the image, and displaying back items on the image by content rendering (head-mounted display [HMD], see-through displays, eyeglasses, contact lens, mobile tablets). AR comprises varied technologies such as SLAM (simultaneous localization and mapping) and depth tracking, also.

2.2.1 Important Concepts Used in AR

a. **Calibration,** tracking, and registration play a very significant role in analyzing the performance of AR systems. The sensors, cameras, and display devices have to collaborate between to have optimal augmentation. Calibration is defined as the procedure of associating and comparing measurements done by various devices (sensors, haptics, displays) with a known reference coordinate system.

b. **Registration** in AR relates to the orientation and alignment of coordinate systems amid virtual computer-generated and real items by tracking the user's head with the camera.

c. **Tracking** is synonymous with "3D tracking" of the 3D position or the six-dimensional pose (position and orientation) of real entities. To project virtual registered objects in 3D space in real time, the location and orientation of the AR display relevant to the real objects must be continuously tracked and updated over time using haptics, sensors, gloves, Wi-Fi wrist bands, Wi-Fi remotes, accelerometers, and compasses.

d. **Computer vision** is used to segment the image and identify the objects of interest that are used to augment the image. Real-time segmentation of the image in 3D space plays an important role in AR. In the current technology, such techniques, together with artificial intelligence, are becoming part of the hardware. Computer vision is also used in haptics to identify and react with gestures.

2.2.2 Types of AR

a. **Marker-based AR:** Capturing, detecting, pose estimating, and tracking a known fiducial marker represented by a mathematical model (square, an image of an electronic component, printed QR code, or special signs) is marker-based AR. Marker tracking is computationally inexpensive and can deliver useful results, even with rather poor cameras. The 3D computer-generated augmented

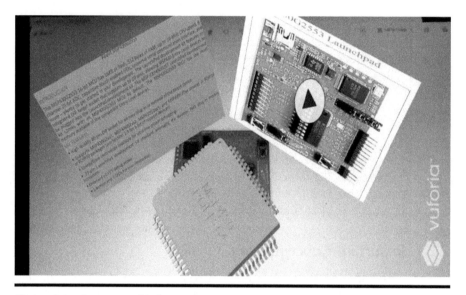

Figure 2.3   Augmented Laboratory.

information will be overlapped in a place relative to the marker. Certain sensors (e.g. GPS, BLE) are used to improve the tracking capability, precision, and speed. As technology evolves, this method will be rarely used in the future. This method is best used for interactive learning from AR Books or AR-enabled product manuals for repairing and also in virtual labs Figure 2.3 is an augmented image and a video which describes an integrated circuit.

b. **Markerless-based AR:** Based on the preexisting 3D models or based on the sensors (Industrial Internet of Things [IIoT], Internet of Things [IoT], compass, gyroscope, accelerometer, database of locations). the augmented image is overlapped over the real-world image. The data obtained from the sensors determines what AR content to place in a certain area of an image. GPS maps with geo-localization are one of the most used applications of AR where the events information, business ad pop-ups, and navigation support are displayed over the maps as shown in Figure 2.4. This method is most popular in interactive games, real estate, and interactive shopping. This is widely used in the industry for local or remote repairing.

c. **Superimposition-based AR:** This is the concept developed for "**Trying before you buy**". This method replaces the original view of any object with a fully or partially augmented projection; 3D surface modeling in real time from image and object recognition plays a key role. In this model, AR permits users to project virtual furniture from a catalog into their house as shown in Figure 2.5. (Matt Reynolds, 2021). This type of AR technology is

Figure 2.4 Pop-Up-Based Navigation-Supported AR.

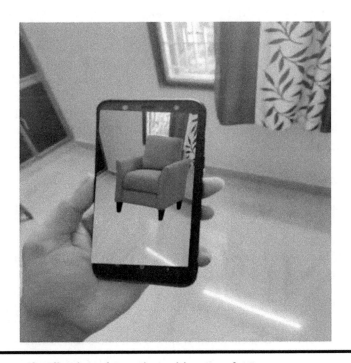

Figure 2.5 Visualization of Superimposition-Based AR.

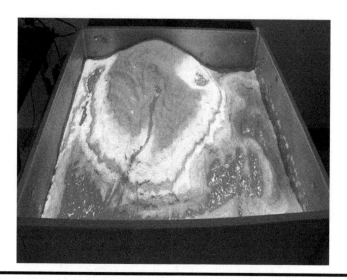

Figure 2.6   Projection-Based AR.

also used for remote repair. Users overlay the 3D model on a product and use the see-through glasses for the training or maintenance instructions.

d. **Projection-Based AR:** This is used for simulation overlay in real time on dynamically changing physical objects. It is used in the education of geography, geology, biology, and chemistry by overlapping reactions to manipulations. This image of a sandbox is reproduced from internet sources explaining contours of elevations while moving the sand by hand. The cameras take images of the surface in real time and overlay the contours by the projector (https://sites.allegheny.edu/bio/2015/02/23/students-get-their-hands-dirty-with-new-augmented-reality-sandbox-2/). This is the best education tool (Figure 2.6).

2.2.3 Hardware

AR hardware can be head-mounted, handheld, or wearable. Some of the popular AR hardware includes mobile phones and tablets; head-up displays (HUD); HMDs (Magic Leap); AR glasses (Vuzix Blade, Google, Apple, Facebook, Optinvent, Everysight Raptor, Epson Moverio, ThirdEye); and AR contact lenses or virtual retinal displays (VRD). Few types of AR glasses are shown in Figure 2.7. The above hardware also consists of 2D, 3D, depth cameras, sensors (GPS, IoT), HMDs, see-through glasses, Magic Loop, handheld display (Renault Config car), stationary display (take an image, overlap objects, and display on TV), projected display (Sandbox), transparent smart window, and audio sets in museums.

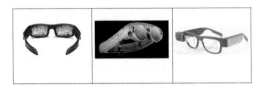

Figure 2.7   Augmented Reality Glasses.

2.2.4 Software

AR applications can be developed easily with the recent software bundles available. A few tools are available to develop the application interactively without any programming. As the market is expanding, more and more tools are available. The tools can be selected based on support for high-level abstraction, loading of 3D models, powerful and fast 3D rendering, support of different media formats, support for open Scene Graph, real-time tracking, interaction with IoT and IIoT, a scripting language (C#, javascript), multiple platforms (Windows, Android, IoS), cloud-based targets and media, efficient computer vision-based image recognition techniques, single or multiple targets in a scene, easy camera calibration, and registration. Finally, the software can be selected based on open source, free, free for academic, or commercial purposes.

The popular software tools available in the market are Metaio, Vuforia, Unity3D with Vuforia, Unity3D with AR Foundation, Wikitude, ARCore, ARKit, MaxST, and Amazon Sumerian. In addition to these standard development tools, other tools may be required for the design of models and special hardware-specific libraries.

2.2.5 AR in Education

The learning process for students needs to be interesting, combined with a sense of creative aspects, and interactive. AR will shortly affect the conventional procedures of learning in educational systems. Many new concepts and methods can be introduced using AR. AR helps classes to be more interactive, interesting, and engaging, and thus enables pupils to learn with joy using exhaustive and progressive learning. AR surely helps in creating an interest in learning.

Due to the wide availability of smartphones and the possibility of integrating the concepts of AR, this technology will revolutionize the education system. AR allows students to obtain additional digital information and provides a process to understand tough information easily. AR can link real and digital content and has been steadily improving, opening more platforms for learners (https://sites.allegheny.edu/bio/2015/02/23/students-get-their-hands-dirty-with-new-augmented-reality-sandbox-2/; Saidin, Halim, & Yahaya, 2015).

Interactive AR enables students to learn abstract concepts through physical form by overlapping 3D models, statistical models, and mathematical models. For example, AR can display X-rays on the human body or a video display of heart functioning on the body. Students can also interact with teachers while doing experiments. Teachers can observe students through AR glasses and send messages via the glasses when students need help. Superimposition-based AR can be used to teach engine/motor assembly along with a physical model and a virtual model (https://unity.com/).

Several commercially available products help students to learn using AR. Some of the products in the market areas follow: Elements 4D by DAQRI Studio is an app for learning chemistry by combining various elements in simulation to see how they react. Anatomy 4D, Corinth Micro Anatomy, and Human Heard 3D display 3D anatomical models of the human body that students can interact with. Math Alive, Animal Alphabet, and Bugs3D are some young student teaching aids that use AR. Many newspapers are coming up with advertisements, news, or images that are AR-enabled and will display more information about the product or news when clicked.

AR is one of the best technologies, and an interactive hybrid learning environment helps to increase conceptual understanding of any phenomenon. One of its most imperative areas is the use of AR applications in teaching, training, etc. that increases the potential of AR to be integrated in education. AR technology introduces virtual objects into real environments, encouraging students to show interest in learning and enhancing visualization of academic concepts. Learning information about any course through AR will be more feasible than learning from the internet or books (https://www.aniwaa.com/guide/vr-ar/ultimate-vr-ar-mr-guide/).

2.2.6 Industrial Applications of AR

The industrial applications are categorized into three major areas based on AR usage:

a. **Complex Assembly:**
The modern assembly of products involves several complex components that need to be put together within a very short time with high precision. AR can provide good assistance with performing these complex assemblies. It can help to push the appropriate information in terms of text, audio, image, or video in the field of hands-free assembly by allowing voice or gesture control. The various commands are broken down into several steps and overplayed on product assembly. With AR, it is also possible to verify the precision of the assembly after each step. AR glasses are useful in such manual assembly, while the workers continue to keep their hands on the task.

b. **Education, Training, and Maintenance:**
AR plays a very crucial role in training and maintenance by replacing the physical manual that may be outdated, or in most cases, the manuals are

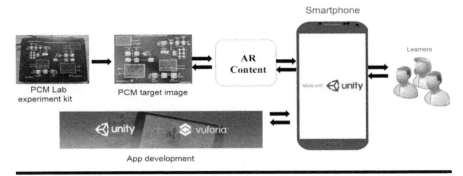

Figure 2.8   Development of AR-Based LAB.

for a group of products of the same category and confuse the customer or technician. The manual process and procedure can be a bit time-consuming and also not completely error free. By using AR based on 3D models of the product, users can learn how to use and maintain the product. AR would permit users to follow the order of usage of the product or the inspection step by step, and inspection results can be sent to experienced analysts so that the usage or maintenance process can be improved (Bazarov, Kholodilin, Nesterov, & Sokhina, 2017; Odeh, Shanab, Anabtawi, & Hodrob, 2013) Figure 2.8 explains the approach for development of AR-based LAB.

c. **Expert Support:**
Most companies have several technical employees but very few experts. If there is a malfunction in the manufacturing process related to any equipment, then an expert has to travel to the worksite to repair it. AR can help reduce travel costs and other expenses by enabling the expert to look into the issue from a remote location. This can be done from anywhere in the world by pushing the instructions to the technician's AR glasses. This AR process can help companies to reduce the cost of experts as well as their time.

2.2.7 Applications of AR

AR is becoming part of everyday life with the use of mobile phones and will grow as HMDs and AR glasses reach more reasonable costs. Below is a non-exhaustive list of possible applications for learning, training, agriculture, shopping, and industry:

a. **Classroom:** Taking automatic attendance, perceiving student actions and reactions, identifying students, teaching with an overlap of models, individual interaction during lab experiments, expert intervention. College admission: Interactive college information. Chemistry experiments: learning periodic tables and chemical reactions. Interactive astronomy and astrology. Learning dance with an overlay of steps and movements. Learning painting and appreciating paintings. Figure 2.9 explains how AR technology can be used in education and medicine.

b. **Agriculture:** Choosing fruits/vegetables ready to pluck, classifying fruits, identifying plant diseases, learning about plants and species (Figure 2.10).

c. **Civil Engineering:** Marketing before construction (real estate), interactive interior decoration, interactive furniture selection and arrangement, wall painting, and decoration (Figure 2.11).

d. **Architecture and Archaeology:** Projecting information at interactive temples and tourist sites, reconstructing destroyed or partially destroyed heritage sites. Living with the past at archaeology sites. Immersing with interactive history, studying rocks, etc. (Figure 2.12).

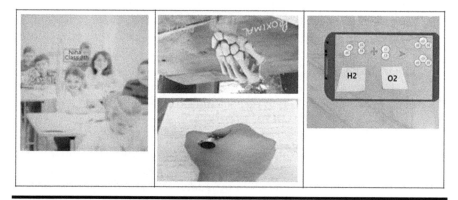

Figure 2.9   AR Technology in Education.

Figure 2.10   AR Technology in Agriculture.

Figure 2.11 **AR Technology in Civil Engineering.**

Figure 2.12 **AR Technology in Archaeology and Architecture.**

Figure 2.13 **AR Technology in Crime Investigation and Security.**

e. **Crime and Security:** Identifying stolen cars, traffic, and security; detecting crime and crime establishment. Advanced navigation and identifying and marking objects in real time in less visible places (military). Reconstructing accidents/incidents (Figure 2.13).

f. **Electronics:** Identifying components. Simulating and animating. Circuit study, circuit modeling, and circuit design. While reading an electronics book, AR applications can help users to learn more about an electronic component (https://developer.vuforia.com/) (Figure 2.14).

g. **Shopping:** Intelligent refrigerators, marketing and sales offers, engaging customers, providing product information and utilization, AR-enabled user guides, product training, remote repair, trying before buying (ornaments, dress) (Figure 2.15).

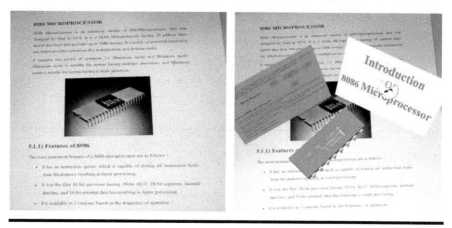

Figure 2.14   User Visualizing Electronic Components Using AR Application in Android.

Figure 2.15   AR Technology in Shopping.

h. **Computer Science:** Learning to program with AR. Writing a program and seeing the simulation.

i. **Automobile, Mechanical:** Interactive car/motor repair, plant maintenance, and engine assembly (https://unity.com/solutions/automotive-transportation-manufacturing) (Figure 2.16).

j. **Physically Disabled:** Hearing aids for blind people, speech to text, walking through streets, shopping aids.

k. **Medicine/Healthcare:** To identify patients, identify disease, diagnose, distance monitoring, interactive physiotherapy, localize the patient. Overlay medical tests (MRI, X-ray, blood tests, etc) results over the body (Figure 2.17).

Figure 2.16   AR Technology in the Automobile Industry.

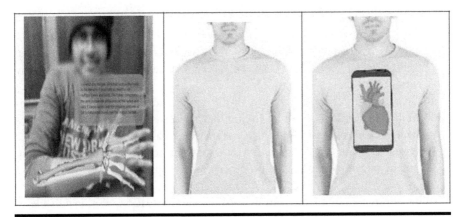

Figure 2.17   AR Technology in Medicine and Healthcare.

l. **Tourism:** Guided visits to temples and places of interest with an overlay of history over places along with a guided map.

m. **Industrial Design:** Interactively design parts and see them virtually overlapping physical products (design a car door for a car, design a window in a wall).

2.3 Virtual Reality

2.3.1 Introduction

VR is an emerging technology that creates a virtual environment for users to enable them to get an aesthetic feel for the desired surroundings. VR technology has varied applications and is useful in advanced sectors such as engineering, medicine, education, entertainment, design, planning, construction, training, and entertainment. VR tries to mimic the real world to give 3D immersive visual and interactive experiences by bringing depth to objects with unlimited 3D space.

AR and VR together will play an important role in the industrial revolution through Education 5.0. They have the potential to develop innovative and desirable solutions in manufacturing, training, and education with the help of smart machines. They use other areas and platforms for high connectivity, networking, and simulation and thus quickly open numerous avenues for technological advancements. VR immersion experience includes 3D simulated images that resemble full-sized pictures from the user's viewpoint and also the ability to track user's interactions (telepresence: head, eyes, and hands) and correspondingly regulate the images on the user's screen to reflect the changes. VR experience creates an illusion and makes the user fully immersed in the virtual world. This is the reason why VR is extensively used to focus on learning and also used in pain therapy.

VR consists of two main components of immersion:

a. Depth of information consists of the amount and quality of the information such as data quality, resolution of the images, complexity of the graphics, and clarity of the audio that a user obtains while interacting in an entirely virtual world.

b. Breadth of information consists of different sensory dimensions that are simultaneously used. A virtual environment that is experienced by a user has a wide breadth of information that has the potential to stimulate all the senses (visual and audio dominate, but it is possible to incorporate the sense of touch, user force feedback, and other similar haptic systems).

VR uses higher frame rate displays with hardware acceleration, so it is possible to explore the life-sized open world environment for the immersion to be effective and be able to change perspectives seamlessly with dynamic change of the point of view according to the user's view. Latency is the lag time amid the user interaction, and change reflection in the virtual world is very important and allows the user to be in the immersion without going back to the real world. A latency of more than 50 milliseconds will destroy the sense of immersion. Such distraction can create motion sickness, called cyber sickness. That is the reason why the input methods are more natural haptic methods like head or eye movement, voice recognition, motion trackers, and a few handheld finger devices along with HMD. VR users experience a greater sense of telepresence during the interaction that is quite interesting, whereas realistic environments often lack openings for interaction and thus cause the handlers to lose interest in learning.

2.3.2 Hardware

VR hardware is a kind of head-mounted closed display unit together with interaction devices that can be with 6DOF (Oculus Quest, HTC Vive) or 3DOF (Oculus Go). The first VR headset, Google Cardboard, was made possible because of the inertial measurement unit (IMU), which measures linear and angular acceleration and position changes using sensor fusion. In recent headsets, IMU is used to measure the movement of the head. The time between moving your head and seeing the virtual world movement is very important to avoid motion sickness. To create such a fast reaction, the GPU plays an important role by creating and rendering high-quality 3D scenes. The availability of such high-performance GPUs makes the VR provide high-fidelity graphics. Some VR devices (HTC Vive) work together with a powerful computer or mobile phone, and some of the recent VR devices (HoloLens, Oculus Go) have the computing power integrated. Microsoft Holo Lens, HoloLens, HTC Vive, and Google Cardboard alt-text Images of various VR hardware are used for visualizing and experiencing virtual reality. Figure 2.18 shows few VR devices used for various applications.

Some of the problems with the VR experience due to hardware are the screen-door effect (visible gaps between pixels), poor latency, inability to adjust inter-pupillary distance, and focus. This may cause motion sickness while experiencing VR.

Figure 2.18   Microsoft HoloLens, HTC Vive, and Google Cardboard.

2.3.3 Virtual Reality Applications

The applications of VR are unlimited and are in every domain of industry, society, and the environment, and especially in the domain of education and training.

  a. **Civil Engineering and Real Estate:** Financers, architects, and prospective customers can walk through a building before finalizing the plans by creating the building virtually. The prospective customers can also view every side of their future habitat, interact with the virtual model, and make alterations to the design. They can also place furniture, color the walls, and perform the interior decoration virtually to their utmost satisfaction. This helps investors to attract prospective customers and satisfy them by making alterations to their satisfaction even before construction (Figure 2.19).
  b. **Biology and Medicine:** Virtual environments are used to educate and train in the medical domain, from surgical procedures to diagnosing patients. A surgery can be carried out remotely by utilizing robots with the help of VR technology, and in Paris at one of the hospitals, the first robotic surgery was performed in 1998 using VR with the support of fine-tuned sensory feedback to the surgeon. Universities and medical institutes use live objects (animals, insects, bodies) to experiment for learning and teaching purposes, but using VR, the learning can be done through 3D models without destroying nature, animals, and insects (https://ossovr.com/) (Figure 2.20).
  c. **Phobias and Pain Therapy:** VR technology is used to treat phobias, stress, post-traumatic stress disorder (PTSD), addiction, pediatric sleep disorders, and other psychological conditions by creating environments virtually as a

Figure 2.19 VR Technology in Civil Engineering and Interior Designing.

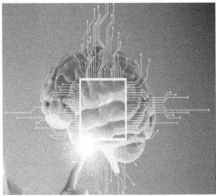

Figure 2.20   VR Technology in Biology and Medicine.

frame for exposure therapy, under controlled conditions that cause a person distress. Because patients know that it is not the actual world, they will be ready to try this therapy just by wearing an HMD (https://www.virtuallybetter.com/).

d. **Virtual Mall/City: Interactive Shopping Experience:** VR can be used to build huge malls and virtually simulate and test different facets of malls like arrangement of shops, design of shops, grouping shops, customer behavior, customer attitude, business peak timings, facilities, employee's availability, and usage. Figure 2.21 is a virtual city developed by a school

Figure 2.21   Building of Cities and Shopping Malls Using Virtual Reality.

student of 9th standard (Tech Unity, 2021). After malls were opened, the data collected from different sources can be pushed back to VR, and the mall could be adjusted according to the needs of the day. With VR technology, one can visit a supermarket virtually, watch the demos of the items required, and select them for purchase. This helps customers to experience the use of the product before buying, which gives satisfaction to customers (Figure 2.21).

e. **VR in Education:** There will be head-on interaction among teachers and students in the classroom before the innovative technologies are integrated with education. This method evinces its effectiveness, but educational institutions are fascinated by introducing more productive methods to enrich learning interaction and enhance the level of confidence, understanding of concepts, and acquisition by learners. The teacher's explanation time can be reduced, students can better visualize concepts, and they can learn with a sense of reality. VR technology is more attractive and demonstrative and creates an interest and a zeal to master the subject. When the quality of the output or task efficiency of an experience is improved for the user, there is no doubt that the future will belong to VR. Thus, VR technology helps replace conventional learning methods and make learning experiences more interactive, reduces the learning and training time of the student, eliminates the limitations caused by physical requirements, and allows students to learn whatever and train themselves wherever, just with an app and headset (Figure 2.22).

f. **Virtual Laboratory:** Physics, chemistry, biology, and engineering experiments can be done interactively using a VR headset without using any

Figure 2.22   VR Technology in Education.

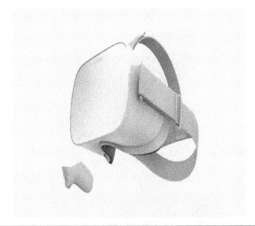

Figure 2.23   Oculus Go VR Head Set.

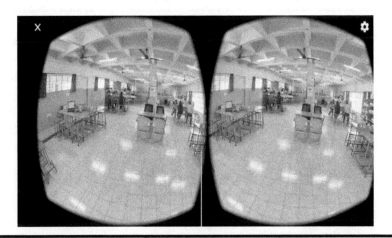

Figure 2.24   User experiencing 360-degree view of a lab of ECE, SVEC in Oculus Go.

physical materials. Such virtual labs help students to repeat experiments based on their knowledge, interest, and learning pace. The same VR models can also be used for evaluations of student learning. Also, the virtually developed laboratories can be interfaced using Oculus Go, VR box Oculus Go, or VR box. The 360-degree view image of the communication lab, SVEC, was captured, and a virtual view was developed using VR technology (http://www.vlab.co.in/) (Figure 2.23 and Figure 2.24).

g. **Training:** Sometimes new employees struggle when they are sent to work on-site or with customers. Better interactive training can be provided to these

Figure 2.25 VR Technology in Training.

employees with the help of VR technology, which is safe and effective. The workers can focus more on their work and raise productivity and can eliminate distractions like noise and other hurdles with the help of virtual training. It is very difficult to produce or simulate real-life problems, but this VR technology helps employees deal with real-time difficulties like an expert (Figure 2.25).

Figure 2.26 VR Technology in Factory Planning.

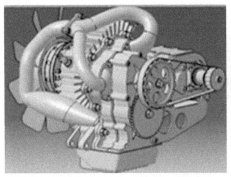 

Figure 2.27 **Engine Assembly and Virtual Lab Environment to Assemble Using Oculus Go.**

h. **Factory Planning:** Immense efforts are required to build a new plant or revamp a current plant. It takes a lot of time and effort to design, redesign, examine, and then conduct trials. Scenarios can be rectified by using VR in virtual plants. Testing can be done any number of times virtually, and flaws in the overall system can be pointed out and rectified with repeated redesigns and virtual testing. The design of the overall plant can be done from scratch, and changes can be done many times virtually. Once satisfied, the plant can be built or revamped in real life (Figure 2.26).

i. **Automobile Industry:** VR technology is used to build virtual designs of new vehicles or parts of vehicles and test them before production. Unlike physical models, virtual models can be altered without any waste, which makes them less expensive and more efficient in the development process. The same virtual models can also be used for VR-based virtual training by the customer or to maintain the vehicle (https://unity.com/). In an engineering college, it is ideal to have virtual labs where students can interact to learn, train, and self-evaluate engine/motor disassembly and assembly without the need for any physical material (https://www.toptal.com/virtual-reality/virtual-reality-in-the-automotive-industry) (Figure 2.27).

2.4 Conclusion and Future Scope

AR and VR help students, learners, teachers, and employees learn and upgrade their knowledge at any time and at any place. AR and VR are useful to help students digest knowledge by associating theory with practical applications and with repetition based on the interest and pace of the learner. It is possible for students to evaluate themselves using the same technology. Gamification helps students to learn with interest by immersion rather than just for learning. It is easy to adapt and develop new applications with little or no programming using pre-defined functions or packages.

AR and VR help an academic organization to update and adapt their skill set to the latest and future needs of society and industry quickly and frequently without much investment as well as follow the standards of Education 5.0 to be ready to adapt to Industry 5.0.

Acknowledgments

Some of the images are taken from associated websites, and we also extend our sincere thanks to the Department of ECE and Mechanical Engineering of Sree Vidyanikethan Engineering College for extending their support to utilize the facilities available in their laboratories.

References

Bazarov, S. E., Kholodilin, Y., Nesterov, A. S., & Sokhina, A. V. (2017). Applying augmented reality in practical classes for an engineering student. *IOP Conference Series: Earth and Environmental Science, 87*, 032004.

https://www.virtuallybetter.com/

https://ossovr.com/: Virtual reality Surgical training.

https://sites.allegheny.edu/bio/2015/02/23/students-get-their-hands-dirty-with-new-augmented-reality-sandbox-2/

https://unity.com/solutions/automotive-transportation-manufacturing

https://www.toptal.com/virtual-reality/virtual-reality-in-the-automotive-industry

https://www.aniwaa.com/guide/vr-ar/ultimate-vr-ar-mr-guide/

https://unity.com/

http://www.vlab.co.in/

https://developer.vuforia.com

https://www.youtube.com/watch?v=3UWCCmPcxMk, 21 Aug 2021.

Liu, D., Dede, C., Huang, R., & Richards, J. (2017). *Virtual, augmented, and mixed realities in education*. Springer, Singapore.

Matt Reynolds (ed.), How IKEA's future-living lab created an augmented reality hit, https://www.wired.co.uk/article/ikea-place-augmented-reality-app-space-10, 21 Aug 2021.

Odeh, S., Shanab, S. A., Anabtawi, M., & Hodrob, R. (2013). A remote engineering lab based on augmented reality for teaching electronics. *International Journal of Online Engineering, 9*.

Saidin, N. F., Halim, N. D. A., & Yahaya, N. (2015). A review of research on augmented reality in education: Advantages and applications. *International Education Studies, 8*.

Chapter 3

Augmented Reality Changing the Food and Beverage Industries

D. Ramya Chitra

Assistant Professor, Department of Computer Science, Bharathiar University, Coimbatore, India

Contents

DOI: 10.1201/9781003175896-3

Objectives

This chapter addresses the following objectives:

1. Revolution of augmented reality (AR) in the food and beverage industries
2. Applications of AR in various sectors of the food and beverage industries
3. Case studies on virtual 3D food, employee training, product–customer interaction, restaurant entertainment, restaurant tours, and product packaging
4. Hardware and software technologies in application development

---

3.1 Introduction

The history of food and beverages is as old as humans, and the development was not up to the mark until the 19th century, with the invention of canning and pasteurization that led to the preservation and packaging of food products. India occupies the third position in the food and beverage industries by market size. The industries use technology to preserve and package food according to the demand of the consumers.[1] In recent years, augmented reality (AR) has brought an essential change in the food and beverage industries. AR that blends the real world and virtual world has several applications. Apart from helping the industries, it also helps end-users by giving a better user experience. It provides a novel way to promote the effectiveness of cuisine; customers can see a live demonstration of cuisine preparation so that they can view food quantity. The users can also see famous restaurants for specific food items using AR applications (apps).

Interaction is helping users to be more involved in AR. Many businesses are trying to upgrade their business model using AR. The development costs of the AR app may be high, but based on the current scenario, the investment in the AR app is worthwhile.

In several eateries, pictures of the food don't represent the qualitative and quantitative measures of the food correctly. Digitization of the old-style published menu will improve the customer's knowledge at the restaurant. Some restaurants offer added incentives and perks for participating in the entertainment offered by the restaurant.

Satisfaction and engagement of the customers towards the product are needed for higher sales. When AR provides accurate information, business owners can improve their standards. Also, AR will create a trusting relationship between clients and business owners (Koui, 2017).

The field of AR has existed for more than one decade, but the growth of the technology has been tremendous and remarkable in just the last few years. AR technology has many applications, including entertainment, engineering (Li, Nee, & Ong, 2017), education (Sirakaya & Alsancak-Sirakaya, 2018), medical training (Barsom, Graafland, & Schijven, 2016), manufacturing, the food industry, construction, archaeology, and sports (Sheikh & Sawant, 2016). AR encourages pupils to discover learning resources from different viewpoints (Kerawalla, Luckin, Selijefot, & Woolard, 2006). In tourism, persons with smartphones fortified with a camera can walk around and learn about the history of places they are visiting. In medicine, a gadget has been made that uses AR to project a picture of the veins onto the skin so that it is easy to trace the veins. Also, doctors can utilize the AR's expertise to discover a patient's surgical incision spot. For psychological disorders, an AR system can be used to reduce anxiety, fear, and avoidance behaviors, and it can also treat specific phobias. In the field of education, AR can be used to overlay audiovisual materials and visuals in the actual setting to show composite molecular structures so that students can learn easily and with more interest. Patients' behavior can be monitored and assessed with AR technology based on their needs (Giglioli, Pallavicini, Pedroli, Serino, & Riva, 2015). AR technology has been used in public security, where drone cameras combine with on-the-ground search teams in the jungle or in street settings for search and rescue operations.

There are many visualization issues caused by the nature of AR technology that have to be considered while developing applications. Registration errors are very important and cannot be avoided. Real objects have to be properly removed from the real environment, and virtual objects have to be properly inserted. AR also offers transparency where mistrust is increasing between consumers and the food industry. The solutions and the services provided by AR help the food industry to go ahead of its competitors and drive sales. Hence, many businesses in the food industry have changed their marketing strategies to have an exceptional position in the competitive field. The AR technology will provide a good opportunity for students with creative skills. In this chapter, many case studies are discussed that may inspire students in their career paths.

3.2 Applications of AR in the Food and Beverage Industries

The application of AR in the food industry is infinite. It has the ability to trigger and monitor consumers' senses. It has made intake awareness virtually pleasing for consumers. Studies were conducted to find the pictorial, sensory, and hepatic essentials for regulating taste insight (Velasco, Carvalho, Petit, & Nijholt, 2018). AR serves as an effective marketing tool in the food and beverage industries, where it is used to increase desire for the product as well as develop interaction with customers (Konopelko, 2019).

With normal packaging, customers can view only restricted information about the product. With AR, information about the product, such as nutritional information, company contact information, etc., can be viewed on consumers' smartphones immediately. AR creates a new marketing dimension for food packaging to improve the sales profits of food businesses. Customer loyalty is also increased, and the companies receive valuable data about buyers. Through this, brand loyalty, social interaction, purchase information, and real-time data analysis provide added value to everyone. Also, to make food education become part of cultural heritage from childhood, many food industries have planned to invest in AR.[2]

AR restaurant menus can be customized to show information such as a 360-degree visualization of the dish, the ingredients used, the nutritional and calorific values, etc. Also, videos of customer testimonials, interviews of chefs, and cooking can be embedded to engage consumers. These menu apps also collect information from customers, which in turn will provide needed information to business owners.[3] Training employees with traditional training materials is time-consuming and expensive. Restaurants are also making use of AR apps to train their staff by helping them to estimate portion size, learn maintenance techniques, etc. Also, training is provided for food safety to avoid illness. AR is very effective in training staff by saving them time and money and hence allows companies to employ a broader range of staff with various needs and learning styles.

Customers can learn about restaurants through three-dimensional (3D) animatronics from published advertising material. Restaurants work together with content-based industries and advertising organizations to build AR-based posters in periodicals. Nutritional information given by AR and other tools were compared and assessed to find whether they affect the choice of healthier food and which app the customer will use in future shopping circumstances. Food information was more comprehensible and prominent when it was shown with traffic light logos compared to nutrition information tables. An AR app was able to improve information saliency, and the AR app was assessed as the most enjoyable method (Csakvary, 2017). The applications of AR for the food and beverage industries are enormous and give positive results. The following sections show some of the industries that have adopted AR.

3.2.1 Virtual 3D Food

New York-based Kabaq (QReal) presents dishes that look real so that users can see the simulated 3D diet on a table in the restaurant as well as through internet shopping. This tool allows users to change the way they present their menu in 3D and to engage with their consumers. This tool is designed to meet the consumer's expectations so that it limits the possibility of confusion. The dishes are photographed from different angles and stitched together to provide 3D models that are added into the Kabaq AR food app. The resulting 3D menu will exist within the restaurant or through the app, which can be accessed anywhere remotely. This tool also gathers data on the consumer's requirements and makes the analytics on the menu selections and developments into food recipes.[4]

FoodGaze is India's first virtual menu that uses virtual 3D food in hotels or online. This extends the visual information without any limit, and consumers can see the food's correct dimensions before they place their order. Consumers can also see the ingredients and nutritional information for any menu item. A Toronto-based startup, 3D Food and Drink, has launched an AR menu system for Canadian Restauranteurs that is delivered across multiple platforms, including Snapchat, Facebook, the Web, and AR. 3D versions of menu items are made by taking hundreds of photos from every angle so that consumers can see menu items from every angle at their exact size either at home or at the restaurant. The techniques that captured the image resulted in reduction in time for capturing hundreds of images from several hours to less than a day (Alan, 2019).

Magnolia Bakery deploys AR technology to virtually render cakes and other items so consumers can feel, touch, and explore their products (Patel, 2020). Bareburger of NYC is using Snapchat's Lens Studio to offer their customers interactive AR images so that users can see what they have ordered, the ingredients, and the portion sizes. Domino's launched an AR-based app called "New Pizza Chef", which allows users to create their favorite pizzas (Sarvaiya, 2020). Jarit, an AR application, allows users to view their order in 3D. Using photogrammetry, 3D images of the dishes are created so that visitors can see their dishes in advance.[5]

3.2.2 Product–Customer Interaction

Nestle has introduced an AR game that is printed in its cereal boxes. Also, Kraft has introduced smart packaging on its consumer packaged goods, and Walmart organized an AR Summer Sweepstakes[6]. Food Network has added AR technology to its cooking app, "In the Kitchen", available on Android. Through this app, Android users can build virtual cupcakes within their surroundings[7]. The Francesco Rinaldi AR app creates a communicating wrapping design, where consumers can directly talk with Mrs. Rinaldi, whose picture is on the container. Consumers with iOS or Android gadgets can use this app to interact with Mrs. Rinaldi (McQuarrie, 2018b). Domino's has developed a pizza hero app where users can make pizzas (Sagar, 2019).

3.2.3 Restaurant Entertainment

Boston's restaurant uses 3D AR games for kids so that families with kids will be attracted to the restaurant. Vida e Caffe, in association with Atlantis, built an AR app, which on scanning will play a video of Atlantis and Dubai playing. Coca-Cola started a Christmas magic campaign, in which users can view a simulated Santa and Christmas pictures when the Coca-Cola can is scanned using the AR in-app camera.[8] Chipotle created a scarecrow game app to engage their customer base (Sagar, 2019).

3.2.4 Employee Training

Restaurants are using AR-based training to teach their staff with videos for cooking delightful meals or making coffee. Google's Daydream Labs has proved that these types of training can improve the learning speed of staff.[9]

3.2.5 AR Restaurant Tours

SMACAR Solutions has integrated an AR game for FoodPath, a multicuisine restaurant located in Mumbai. Here, the customers can get discount offers by playing the AR game by scanning the client's emblem on published resources such as leaflets, menu cards, and the logo on their website. It also provides an interactive experience, and users can learn about the promotional materials.[9] Sam's Club, the retail warehouse of Walmart, is using mobile checkout for consumers who use Scan and Go technology for shopping. This app gives information on AR product packaging as well as moving around the store using a custom-made map. Also, the app can be used for ordering items online (McQuarrie, 2018c).

Hub Hotel has an interactive wall map so that tourists can scan the app from their phone and find the attractions nearby. Marriot Hotels, in association with Blippar, has produced interactive ads in their magazine, where users can scan the advertisement to unlock a video. In addition, Pokemon Go is used by many restaurants to lure consumers.[10] Yelp's Monocle app searches and exhibits nearby hotels and services on the screen using a smartphone camera, compass, and GPS. Customers can select any restaurant and view a map to the restaurant as well as view the reviews about the restaurant with AR (Sagar, 2018).

3.2.6 AR for Food Packaging

AR packaging helps to deliver an exclusive experience to users. This packaging improves the profile of the company and also increases sales of the product. The smartphone app allows customers to learn about the brand (Gupta, 2019). Win-a-box employs AR to describe the advantages of potable water, and consumers can interact with the product in a distinctive way. It helps consumers to learn the worth of the product, how to use it, how is it accumulated, and its functions (Roberge, 2018). McDonald's used AR for packaging French fries during the 2014 World Cup; a soccer game was generated on the French fry packaging using AR technology (Aimee, 2018).

Lacta's chocolate packaging wrapper contains a secret message with a marker that can be observed using a mobile device. The user's message can be shown on a mobile screen – someone that the person cares about on a birthday or other occasion (McQuarrie, 2014). The bottom label of Appletiser, a South African flavored sparkling water brand, can be scanned for a different combination of AR experiences based on three personalities the company has launched (Byers, 2015). My Yeti's ice cream wrappers have AR cartoons featuring a cast of characters, like a family of snow people, that are assigned to different ice cream products; kids can join in the adventures (McQuarrie, 2018a).

3.3 Technologies Used and Impact on Industries

The significant technologies of AR include intelligent display technology, 3D registration technology, and intelligent interaction technology. Three main classes of display devices play a significant role in the use of AR technology. The helmet display, modeled in 1968, superimposes simple images generated by processors on actual scenarios in the physical environment. The second AR display is the handheld device display that is light and small. The third display, the personal computer desktop monitor, will match the actual information seized by the camera to a 3D simulated model and exhibit it on the monitor. 3D registration technology permits simulated images to be overlaid precisely in the actual environment. There are many ways of 3D registration based on hardware tracker, computer vision, wireless network, and mixed registration technology (Liddle, 2007). In AR systems, hardware device interactions, location interactions, and tag-based interactions are available (Chen et al., 2019). These can co-exist, and the technical issues are succeeded by experiential, user-focused, and human–computer interaction. AR can be accessed from (i) mobile devices like smartphones or tablets; (ii) head-mounted displays, glasses, and lenses; or (iii) PC and connected TV players.

To combine virtual and real environments, several tools have to be assembled with technological processes, such as computer graphics and computer vision. In the registration process, location coordinates are overlapped with virtual objects, by which the said objects are combined with the real world. For this, code recognition for initiation of the process, markers or images for observation, and spatial orientation are needed. The specific procedure to be considered for this is tracking through video, localization sensors, magnetic sensors, etc. (Azuma, 1997).

Mapping of images will be performed in the calibration process, where surface geometry and latency time are significant. 3D objects are projected into the surroundings based on scale and perspective in the rendering process and the simulated items are combined in the real situation in the visualization process (Azuma et al., 2001). GPS, ultrasonic, mechanical, inertia, and electromagnetic motion tracking are the main tracking-based technologies used in AR, where each tracking system rests on the type of structure being established (Etonam, Gravio, Kuloba, & Nijri, 2019).

Many mobile AR applications use locations, and to attain this the phone must be equipped with GPS technology, an accelerometer, and a digital compass (Yuen,

Yaoyuneyong, & Erik Johnson, 2011). The integration of hardware and software is needed in the initial stage of the plan procedure. To design the system, factors such as the number of users, availability of internet, size limitation, robust nature of the system, throughput requirement of the system, etc. need to be considered.

The software used to develop the applications is AR visualization software, AR content management system, AR software development kit, AR WYSIWYG editor software, industrial AR platforms, AR training simulator software, AR game engine software, etc. The software should be able to manage all the contents that have been created within the platform. The software should permit the user to modify the content, regulate the colors and pictures, and add whatever particulars are needed. The software used in AR must be able to integrate with the hardware, such as mobile phones, glasses, tablets, etc. (Etonam et al., 2019). To reduce the error rate, different visual effects can be used so that the test security, reliability, and reality of the system can be improved. Simulation and evaluation of different circumstances are designed to increase the efficiency of the application in the development stage (Hsu, Wang, Jiang, & Wei., 2015).

An authoring system for context-aware AR is developed that delivers ideas as well as methods for the applications, and users can organize text, images, and CAD models and also relate the AR contents with maintenance contexts (Zhu, Ong, & Nee, 2015). The category of software used for AR systems ranges from low-level programming libraries to higher level AR applications. The software directly used for creating AR applications is environmental acquisition, sensor integration, application engine, and rendering software. In this, the software will perform the tracking function, driving the displays, etc. The software used to create content is also used here (Craig, 2013). We will review some of the techniques and algorithms used in the AR system.

The augmentations have to be combined realistically, and the software must be able to determine the real-world coordinates autonomous of the camera and the graphics. To detect the interest points, feature detection methods, such as corner detection, edge detection, blob detection methods, and other image processing methods, are used. The real-world coordinate system from the interest points is restored using methods like projective geometry, geometric algebra, non-linear optimization, robust statistics, etc. An AR via expert demonstration authoring tool was developed, which determines various calibration parameters and records and processes the assembly demonstration and refining orientation and positions of 3D models (Yulia et al., 2018).

Enhanced hybrid recursive matching and λ-parameterization techniques have been developed to enhance the conception of the images. Also, a mean shift filter is used to enhance the similarity process in image registration. These algorithms were able to solve visualization issues that were caused by neighboring and hidden parts in liver and bowel surgeries (Singh et al., 2019). A projective AR system was developed to transform the visual features of foods or plates into digital mode. Psychophysical experiments were conducted to explore how the taste of food can be modified (Nishizawa, Jiang, & Okajima, 2016). Modification of the visual features influenced sensory attributes, such as consistency and taste of ketchup, so that various skewness led consumers to think they were tasting different kinds of ketchup (Huisman, Bruijnes, & Heylen, 2016).

The role of an audition that the consumers may hear at the time they eat is also used in the AR system. The sounds may be the ones that consumers have when they have interaction with the food and also sounds from the surroundings. A multisensory framework is designed, and the organized connections among the senses provide the framework for the combination of sounds during eating (Velasco et al., 2016). The view of flavor can be influenced by touching or feeling when eating or drinking. It is found that haptically and visually perceived texture can impact the oral-somatosensory judgments of texture and the taste and flavor of diet. For this, the tactile aspects of packaging design, as well as servicer, have to be noted (Biggs, Juravle, & Spence, 2016). Multisensory factors that affect taste, flavor, and smell for typical and atypical populations and tactile taste communications in the general population experiment are discussed. The discovery of tastes inside the flavors may be influenced by higher level cross-sensory cues between different perceptions (Slocombe, Carmichael, & Simner, 2016).

Gravitamine Spice has been developed to emphasize cross-modal interaction. Here, a fork-type device has been developed by using an accelerometer, photo reflector sensor, and motor slider to control the center of gravity and weight of the utensil in digital form (Hirose et al., 2015). A haptic display based on the sensitivity of lips is generated, which is a high-resolution tactile interface for the lips, where vibrotactile stimuli using piezo bimorph cells have been presented that generated a new interactive design space (Tsutsui, Hirota, Nojima, & Ikei, 2016). Virtual drinking sensation of the mouth and lips has been presented where, due to the high sensitivity of the mouth and lips when used as a sensor, development of a unique interface can be made. This might help consumers to almost experience the feeling of drinking (Hashimoto et al., 2006).

A simple mobile educational application using AR resources has been proposed, which uses different image processing techniques like text recognition, marker-based, markerless, and cloud-based model tracking. In this model, the user, by keeping the camera over the page, can get the augmented information. Through this model, children can learn concepts using graphical aids that are described using a 3D model that can be viewed at all angles (Singh & Saikia, 2018).

An outdoor markerless AR system was proposed that considers the mobility of users to target buildings where 3D virtual objects can be augmented. This system makes use of local feature-based image registration technology and Structure from Motion that will regenerate the 3D models using photographs. The positional relationship between 3D virtual objects and real-world scenarios has to be recognized precisely (Satu, Fukuda, Yabuki, Michikawa, & Motamedi, 2016). Different visual features for AR-based assembly directions were identified. The visual features that were used to describe a specific assembly operation have to agree to its difficulty level; hence, various types of visual structures were associated with various levels of task complexity (Radkowski, Herrama & Oliver, 2015).

An AR app has been developed to help understand the data about carbohydrates in real wrapped foods so that markers are not needed. The entire package is tracked by the app and helps the user to detect the surface of the real bundle where the data about carbohydrates is found. Unity and Vuforia Engine have been used for the development of the app. The limitations that have been identified for this app are sample profile and size (Juan, Charco, Garcia-Garcia, & Molla, 2019). The information on product attributes, like carbon footprint information, was provided through AR displays on bottled water and breakfast cereal. It was found that a 23% reduction in carbon footprint was obtained for bottled water and non-significant reductions in breakfast cereal. AR-informed choice led to better cereal procurements that help in decision making and lead to better choices (Isley, Ketcham, & Arent, 2017). The requirements of the holographic display based on the development of LCD that includes resolution, viewing angle, image quality, and the backlight was studied. An initial way for the usage of LCD to progress AR technology is discussed. The integration of virtual images and real scenes can be obtained by applying the holographic technique to AR devices. An exactly controlled phase modulator with compensated feedback algorithm can be used to achieve better results (Lin & Wu, 2017).

AR is used to support the repetitive operations performed in Danish Slaughterhouse facilities, mainly to trim operations. The operation consists of trimming and cutting pork bellies, the most used procedure in the pork meat industry. Due to the biological variability of the pigs, final products vary in yield, even though the final qualities of the product are similar. When AR is applied to cutting operations, it increases the production yield. The operators also need training to benefit from the application. Creator Software Suite and Junaio display channel is used for this application. The 3D maps are made from CT scanning of the raw material. The 3D surface is mapped to 2D trackable using a supervised semiautomatic process, and a connection will be created among the tracked meat and artificial augmentation (Christensen & Engell-Norregard, 2016).

Inaccurate counting of carbohydrates for the treatment of diabetes will result in errors that may lead to complications in glycemic control. A smartphone application that is used to find the number of carbohydrates was used by a group of patients. For evaluating, a test that measures carbohydrate estimation was planned and completed. Interference with smartphone applications to help carbohydrate estimation is comparatively accurate (Domhart, Tiefengrabner, & Dinic, 2015). An AR game that supports therapeutic education for patients with diabetics was presented. This application helped children learn the content of carbohydrates in different foods, and virtual foods of the real dish were shown. It was found that the children showed interest in learning the carbohydrate choices using the game. Unity Engine and Vuforia SDK were used, through which animated objects and very complex virtual objects were included. Blender software was used to create 3D models. For this app, children needed only a minimum setup with some pictures published on paper and a handheld device (Calle Bustos, Juan, Garcia, & Abad, 2017).

An interactive AR application was developed to explain the notions of enzyme kinetics. It took the students to various locations on campus to view videos. This helped the students to prepare for a mock interview. This type of technology can be used to teach difficult concepts and help ease the drain on administrative budgets from multiple wet labs (Crandall et al., 2015). An AR tool of traditional Sundanese food named Ma'Ugiz for nutrition education was developed for teenagers. Unity 3D was used to develop this app. By using this, the users had a lot of opportunities to explore the food preparation procedures as well as the nutrition information. 3D objects were created for this app using blender software. WonderShare Filmora software was used to create videos. The authors believed that nutrition education would introduce the values of wisdom, which would play a major role in character education to encourage the students to love their culture. The education media that was developed was in the form of a book. The pages of the book consisted of several pictures of the traditional book, which functioned as markers for the application (Singh et al., 2019).

The impact of AR mobile application on the learning inspiration of UG health students at the University of Cape Town was studied. The investigation tested the differences before and after using the AR mobile application for student learning motivation. It was found that the attention, satisfaction, as well as confidence factors of the students were increased (Khan, Johnston, & Ophoff, 2019). A framework has been proposed for supporting maintenance services in the food industry using mobile devices and AR technologies. The tasks to be carried out are represented using 3D visual instructions using AR that would be visible through a mobile device. The work of the monitor can be observed from a remote location. The supervisor will have to collaborate with the operator by transferring warnings that are noticeable to the operator in the augmented environment (Re & Bordegoni, 2014).

AR markers for obtaining 3D images of all the dishes on a menu use joint properties of QR codes and AR by scanning the QR code connected with the particular eatery menu. The health constituent of the dish, taste, servings, etc. will be presented, and the traditional menu ordering process can be eliminated. For this, a trackable image is designed, and the region is marked where the actual QR content label is available (Harekal, Veena, Goyal, & Sinha, 2019). Some of the tools that are available to create AR applications are Daqri, MixAR, and ZooBrust, which do not require any programming ability. Other tools available are ARToolKit, Unifeye Mobile SDK, and Wikitude, which let developers design various AR applications for different devices.

AR technology has a optimistic influence on the food industry as it improves new employee training; helps remove errors in food processing; eases the learning curve for food preparation; brings new efficiencies to warehousing and fruit and vegetable picking and packing; and boosts customer, worker, and food safety. Animal slaughtering, as well as processing in the food industry, are dangerous workplaces where the industry has experienced fatal injuries. AR provides a new kind of training experience for food and beverage industry employees. The employers who adopted these technologies claim that an 80% retention rate has been achieved one year after the employee has been trained (Nichols, 2019). AR finds good solutions for manufacturing errors. As the product prototyping can be digitized in 3D, it is easy to access and redesign the model. Business leaders can make the apt choice at the right time, and the team can act effectively and efficiently so that the overall experience and profit can be enhanced. Also, as AR gives the nutritional information and ingredients of food and beverage items, it allows chefs to try new recipes that customers would like to try. AR is also increasing the engagement and efficiency of the process by creating an AR projection on call at the other end, and it makes the users feel as if they are talking directly to businesses (Rai, 2019).

Artificial intelligence (AI) can be used in the food industry to save food and drink production costs. It is expected to save 20% to 50% of cleaning time for the food industry. It can also be used for managing the food shelves in supermarkets by giving owners information on the most in-demand products. It can be used to plan menus based on diners' food preferences. It will be used to lessen food waste by giving information on what users prefer. Based on users' reviews of their taste preferences, AI can develop new recipes (Mehta, 2018).

3.4 Conclusion and Future of Food

AR is used in very interesting and state-of-the-art ways. AR technology can modify the research landscape in consumption, biometrics, food structure and texture, sensory marketing, and augmenting sensory perception. Asia Pacific will emerge as the largest market for AR by the end of 2024. AR is changing the world of food for the better, compared to the previous strategies followed. There has been a massive transformation and advancement in the food industry due to the adoption of AR. AR has the potential to provide learners with contextual information to enhance learning experiences in the field. Educational experiences will continue to increase in AR in the coming years as AR brings flexibility to on-the-job training. When AR is used, it will help industries to cut training costs by delivering the best quality of training possible. AR is helpful for industries as well as consumers in the aspects of packaging, quality control, marketing, attracting consumers, etc. Food packaging may involve sonic technologies in the future as sounds can influence sensory expectations connected with food. Many leading food industries have used AR and have had good user response and success. To increase the customer's reach and gain momentum in the market, adoption of AR is needed.

There are some challenges to be considered while developing AR apps. There is a lack of development standards, and implementation of technical standards is quite complex and expensive. As the initial costs of development are higher, only a few food and beverage industries are adopting AR technology. Due to the inconsistencies in AR programming and negligence, there is a chance of getting into trouble over privacy and security. There is a possibility of physical harm to the user and the surroundings as AR acts in the real world with some digital overlays. Even though some challenges will be encountered during the development of AR applications, AR technology has proven its capability of extending the experience of users and making life more convenient. Changes in consumer desires are coming fast, and commercial models are needed to support the innovation. The food production system in the future will lessen waste and expand the food base. The future of the food industry will provide several options and convenience to users. When AI is combined with AR, delivery efficiency will be maximized, customer interactions will be handled to the maximum satisfaction and drive the recommendations, etc. Also, the technology will help users to choose healthy eating options by connecting their eating habits with doctor-prescribed diets. Thus, the rapid advances in technology will fuel the consumer's expectations that will be provided in response to their needs and demands. Also, this technology, in the context of education, will give students splendid opportunities in their career paths.

Notes

1. Food and Beverage Industry in India and Abroad-Overview, Market Size, Growth Trends, News Resources. http://www.careerizma.com/industries/food-and-beverage/, [accessed on 7 April 2020].
2. Smart Packaging: Augmented Reality Packaging. https://www.interpack.com/en/ TIGHTLY _PACKED/SECTORS/FOOD_INDUSTRY_PACKAGING/News/Smart_ Packaging_Augmented_Reality_Packaging, [accessed on 7 April 2020].
3. Augmented Reality Menu. https://www.juegostudio.com/ar-based-food-menu-case-study, [accessed on 7 April 2020].
4. Bringing your restaurant menu to life is the future of food ordering. https://www.kabaq.io/use-case/detail/bringing-your-restaurant-menu-to-life-is-the-future-of-food-ordering, [accessed on 7 April 2020].
5. JARIT is an AR Garnish For Your Menu. https://jarit.app/, [accessed on 08 April 2020].
6. Have You Read? Augmented Reality in Food and Beverages Industry Is Your Best Bet to Grow. https://augray.com/blog/have-you-heard-augmented-reality-in-food-beverages-industry-is-your-best-bet-to-grow/, [accessed on 9 April 2020]
7. Network's "In the Kitchen" App Adds an Augmented Reality Feature to its Android App, 2018. https://corporate.discovery.com/discovery-newsroom/food-networks-in-the-kitchen-app-adds-an-augmented-reality-feature-to-its-andriod-app/, [accessed on 9 April 2020].

8. Augmented and Virtual Reality, The Real Appetizers Reshaping Food Industry. https://prismetric.weebly.com/blog/augmented-and-virtual-reality-the-real-appetizers-reshaping-food-industry, [accessed on 9 April 2020].
9. Augmented Reality Case Studies for Restaurants. https://smacar.com/augmented-reality-case-study-restaurants-case-study-restaurants/, [accessed on 9 April 2020].
10. Augmented Reality in Tourism. https://thinkmobiles.com/blog/augmented-reality-tourism/, [accessed on 10 April 2020].

References

Alan, S. (2019). 3d food and drink – Augmented reality menus come to life at restaurants canada show 2019. https://www.linkedin.com/pulse/3d-food-drink-alan-smithson, [accessed on 8 April 2020].

Azuma, R. (1997). A survey of augmented reality. *Presence Teleoperators Virtual Environment*, *6*(4), 355–385.

Azuma, R., Baillot, Y., Bchringer, R., Feiner, S., Julier, S., & MacIntyrc, B. (2001). Recent advances in augmented reality. *IEEE Computer Graphics Applications*, *21*(6), 34–47. doi: 10.1111/1541-4329.12048

Barsom, E. Z., Graafland, M., & Schijven, M. P. (2016). Systematic review on the effectiveness of augmented reality applications in medical training. *Surgical Endoscopy*, *30*(10), 4174–4183. doi: 10.1007/s00464-016-4800-6

Biggs L., Juravle G., & Spence C. (2016). Haptic exploration of plateware alters the perceived texture and taste of food. *Food Quality and Preference*, *50*, 129–134. doi: 10.1016/j.foodqual.2016.02.007

Byers, R. (2015). A limited edition appletiser boasts an augmented reality bottle. https://www.trendhunter.com/trends/augmented-reality-bottle, [accessed on 10 April 2020].

Calle Bustos, A. M., Juan, M. C., Garcia I. G., & Abad, F. (2017). An augmented reality game to support therapeutic education for children with diabetes. *PLoS ONE*, *12*(9). doi: 10.1371/journal.pone.0184645

Chen, Y., Wang, Q., Chen, H., Song, X., Tang, H., & Tian, M. (2019). An overview of augmented reality technology. *Journal of Physics: Conference Series*, *1237*. ICSP 2019 022082.

Christensen, L. B., & Engell-Norregard, M. P. (2016). Augmented reality in the slaughterhouse—A future operation facility. *Food Science and Technology*, *2*(1). doi: 10.1080/23311932.2016.1188678

Craig, A. B. (2013). *Understanding augmented reality—Concepts and applications*. Morgan Kaufmann. Waltham, USA, 297

Crandall, P. G., Engler, R. K.III, Beck, D. E., Killian, S. A., O'Bryan, C. A., Jarvis, N., & Clausen, E. (2015). Development of an augmented reality game to teach abstract concepts in food chemistry. *Journal of Food Science Education*, *14*(1), 18–23.

Csakvary, B. (2017). Promoting healthier food choices with the application of Augmented Reality (MSc Thesis, Wageningen University). 89 pp.

Domhart, M., Tiefengrabner, M., & Dinic, R. (2015). Training of carbohydrate estimation for people with diabetes using mobile augmented reality. *Journal of Diabetes Science and Technology*, *9*(3), 516–524. doi: 10.1177%2F1932296815578880

Etonam, A. K., Gravio, G. D., Kuloba, P. W., & Nijri, J. G. (2019). Augmented reality (AR) application in manufacturing encompassing quality control and maintenance.

International Journal of Engineering and Advanced Technology, *9*(1), 197–204. doi: 10.35940/ijeat.A1120.109119

Giglioli, I. A. C., Pallavicini, F., Pedroli, E., Serino, S., & Riva, G. (2015). Augmented reality: A brand new challenge for the assessment and treatment of psychological disorders. *Advances in Computational Psychometrics*, 2015, 1–12. doi: https://doi.org/10.1155/2015/862942

Gupta, J. (2019). Augmented reality packaging solution for food and beverage industry. Available at: https://www.quytech.com/blog/augmented-reality-food-packaging/, [accessed on 10 April 2020].

Harekal, D., Veena, G. S., Goyal, A., & Sinha, R. (2019). Reaug an implemented augmented reality enabled scanner for restaurants. *International Journal of Innovative Technology and Exploring Engineering*, *8*(8S3) 1–4.

Hashimoto, Y., Nagaya, N., Kojima, M., Miyajima, S., Ohtaki, J., Yamamoto, A., ..., Inami, M. (2006). *Straw-like user interface: Virtual experience of the sensation of drinking using a straw.* In: Proceedings of the 2006 ACM SIGCHI International Conference on Advances in Computer Entertainment Technology (ACE '06), New York, NY: ACM. doi: 10.1145/1178823.1178882

Hirose, M., Iwazaki, K., Nojiri, K., Takeda, M., Sugiura, Y., & Inami, M. (2015). *Gravitamine spice: A system that changes the perception of eating through virtual weight sensation.* In Proceedings of the 6th Augmented Human International Conference (AH '15), New York, NY: ACM, 33–40. doi: 10.1145/2735711.2735795

Hsu, K.-S., Wang, C.-S., Jiang, J.-F., & Wei, H.-Y. (2015). Development of a real-time detection system for augmented reality driving, mathematical problems in engineering. *Macroscopic/Mesoscopic Computational Material Science Modeling and Engineering*, 2015, 1–5. doi: 10.1155/2015/913408

Huisman, G., Bruijnes, M., & Heylen, D. K. J. (2016). *A moving feast: Effects of color, shape and animation on taste associations and taste perceptions.* In Proceedings of the 13th International Conference on Advances in Computer Entertainment Technology (ACE 2016), New York, NY: ACM, 12. doi: 10.1145/3001773.3001776

Isley, S. C., Ketcham, R., & Arent, D. J. (2017). Using augmented reality to inform consumer choice and lower carbon footprints. *Environmental Research Letters*, *12*(6), 1–8. doi: 10.1088/1748-9326/aa6def

Juan, M. C., Charco, J. L., Garcia-Garcia, I., & Molla, R. (2019). An augmented reality app to learn to interpret the nutritional information on labels of real packaged foods. *Frontiers of Computer Science*, *1*(1), 1–16. doi: 10.3389/fcomp.2019.00001

Kerawalla, L., Luckin, R., Selijefot, S., & Woolard, A. (2006). Making it real: Exploring the potential of augmented reality for teaching primary school science. *Virtual Reality*, *10*, 163–174. doi: 10.1007/s10055-006-0036-4

Khan, T., Johnston, K., & Ophoff, J. (2019). The impact of an augmented reality application on learning motivation of students. *Personal Assistance and Monitoring Devices Applications*, *2019*(2), 1–14. doi: 10.1155/2019/7208494

Konopelko, M. (2019). Augmented Reality packaging in food and beverage industry (Thesis, Degree Program in International Business, Saimaa University of Applied Sciences). 64 pp.

Koui, E. (2017). AvantI'appetit: An augmented reality interactive menu that elevates the gourmet food experience (M.F.A thesis, Rochester Institute of Technology, RIT Scholar Works). 63 pp.

Li, W., Nee, A. Y. C., & Ong, S. K. (2017). A state-of-the-art review of augmented reality in engineering analysis and simulation. *Multimodal Technologies and Interaction*, *1*(17). doi: 10.3390/mti1030017.

Liddle, D. (2007). Adopting technology. In B. Moggridge (Ed.), *Designing interactions* (pp. 237–257). Cambridge, MA: MIT Press.

Lin, H. C., & Wu, Y.-H. (2017). Augmented reality using holographic display. *Optical Data Processing and Storage*, *3*, 101–106.

McQuarrie, L. (2014). Lacta's chocolate packaging wrapper hides secret messages with AR. https://www.trendhunter.com/trends/chocolate-packaging-wrapper, [accessed on 10 April 2020].

McQuarrie, L. (2018a). My Yeti's ice cream packaging design engages kids with augmented reality. https://www.trendhunter.com/trends/ice-cream-wrapper, [accessed on 10 April 2020].

McQuarrie, L. (2018b). The Francesco Rinaldi AR app creates an interactive packaging design. https://www.trendhunter.com/trends/interactive-packaging-design, [accessed on 9 April 2020].

McQuarrie, L. (2018c). 'Sam's Club Now' introduces a mobile-first shopping experience. https://www.trendhunter.com/trends/sams-club-now, [accessed on 9 April 2020].

Mehta, A. (2018). AI, AR and VR: The three elements that are making your food technical. https://appinventiv.com/blog/three-elements-that-are-making-your-food-technical/, [accessed 12 April 2020].

Nichols, M. R. (2019). How will AR and VR improve safety in the food industry?. https://foodsafetytech.com/column/how-will-ar-and-vr-improve-safety-in-the-food-industry/, [accessed 12 April 2020].

Nishizawa, M., Jiang, W., & Okajima, K. (2016). *Projective-AR system for customizing the appearance and taste of food*. In: Proceedings of the 2016 Workshop on Multimodal Virtual and Augmented Reality (MVAR '16),New York, NY: ACM, 6. doi: 10.1145/3001959.3001966

Patel, R. (2020). AR/VR in restaurants: Unveiling its benefits, challenges and use cases. https://aglowiditsolutions.com/blog/ar-vr-in-restaurants/, [accessed on 08 April 2020].

Radkowski, R., Herrama, J., & Oliver, J. (2015). Augmented reality-based manual assembly support with visual features for different degrees of difficulty. *International Journal of Human-Computer Interaction*, *31*(5), 337–349. doi: 10.1080/10447318.2014.994194

Rai, T. (2019). Augmented reality examples: 10 industries using AR to reshape business. https://www.clickz.com/augmented-reality-examples-10-industries-using-ar-to-reshape-business/214953/, [accessed 12 April 2020]

Re, G. M., & Bordegoni, M. (2014). An augmented reality framework for supporting and monitoring operators during maintenance tasks. In R. Shumaker, & S. Lackey (Eds.), *Virtual, augmented and mixed reality, applications of virtual and augmented reality, VAMR 2014, Published in:Lecture Notes in Computer Science* (Vol. 8526, pp. 443–454). Cham: Springer.

Roberge, D. (2018). Take your packaging to the next level with augmented reality. https://www.industrialpackaging.com/blog/take-your-packaging-to-the-next-level-with-augmented-reality, [accessed on 10 April 2020].

Sagar, P. (2018). Why restaurants should create an augmented reality app. https://www.digitaldoughnut.com/articles/2018/august/why-should-restaurants-decide-to-create-an-ar-app, [accessed on 10 April 2020].

Sagar, P. (2019). Augmented reality: A technology, restaurants are adopting for increasing customers. https://arvrjourney.com/augmented-reality-a-technology-restaurants-are-adopting-for-increasing-customers-a3c600fac464, [accessed on 9 April 2020].

Sarvaiya, D. (2020). The delectable benefits of augmented reality in restaurants. https://www.intelivita.co.uk/blog/benefits-of-augmented-reality-in-restaurants, [accessed on 8 April 2020].

Satu, Y., Fukuda, T., Yabuki N., Michikawa, T. & Motamedi, A. (2016). *A marker-less augmented reality system using image processing the techniques for architecture and urban environment.* In 21st International Conference of the Association for Computer Aided Architectural design research in Asia, HongKong, pp. 713–722.

Sheikh, A., & Sawant, K. (2016). Introduction to augmented reality: An overview, development of AR in android. *International Journal of Advanced Research in Computer Engineering and Technology*, 5(6), 1989–1994.

Singh, K. J., & Saikia, L. P. (2018). Implementation of image processing using augmented reality. *International Research Journal of Engineering and Technology*, 5(6), 1292 – 1296.

Singh, T., Alsadoon, A., Prasad, P. W. C., Alsadoon, O. H., Venkata, H. S., & Alrubaie, A. (2019). A novel enhanced hybrid recursive algorithm: Image processing based augmented reality for gall bladder and uterus visualization. *Egyptian Informatics Journal*, 21(2), July 2020, 1–14. doi: 10.1016/j.eij.2019.11.003

Sirakaya, M., & Alsancak-Sirakaya, D. (2018). Trends in educational augmented reality studies: A systematic review. *Malaysian Online Journal of Educational Technology*, 6, 60–74. doi: 10.17220/mojet.2018.02.005

Slocombe, B. G., Carmichael, D. A., & Simner, J. (2016). Cross-modal tactile–taste interactions in food evaluations. *Neuropsychologia*, 88, 58–64. doi: 10.1016/j.neuropsychologia.2015.07.011

Tsutsui, Y., Hirota, K., Nojima, T., & Ikei, Y. (2016). High-resolution tactile display for lips. In: S. Yamamoto (Ed.), *Human interface and the management of information: Applications and services. HIMI 2016, Published in: Lecture notes in computer science* (Vol. 9735, pp. 357–366). Berlin: Springer.

Velasco, C., Carvalho, F. R., Petit, O., & Nijholt, A. (2016). *A multisensory approach for the design of food and drink enhancing sonic systems.* In A. Nijholt, C. Velasco, Huisman G., & K. Karunanayaka (Eds.), Proceedings of the 1st Workshop on Multi-sensorial Approaches to Human-Food Interaction (MHFI '16), New York, NY: ACM, 7. doi: 10.1145/3007577.3007578

Velasco, C., Obrist, M., Petit, O., & Spence, C. (2018). Multisensory technology for flavor augmentation: A mini review. *Frontiers in Psychology*, 9 (26). doi: 10.3389/fpsyg.2018.00026

Weber, A. (2018). Trend Alert: Augmented reality in package design. Available at: https://info.mrpcap.com/blog/trend-alert-augmented-reality-in-package-design, [accessed on 10 April 2020].

Yuen, S. C.-Y., Yaoyuneyong, G., & Johnson, E. (2011). Augmented reality: An overview and five directions for AR in education. *Journal of Educational Technology Development and Exchange*, 4(1), 119–140. doi:10.18785/jetde.0401.10

Yulia, C., Hasbullah, H., Nikmawati, E. E., Mubaroq, S. R., Abullah, C. U., & Widiaty, I. (2018). Augmented reality of traditional food for nutrition education. *MATEC Web of Conferences*, 197(2) 16001. doi: 10.1051/matecconf/201819716001

Zhu, J., Ong, S. K., & Nee, A. Y. C. (2015). A context-aware augmented reality assisted maintenance system. *International Journal of Computer Integrated Manufacturing*, 28(2), 213–225. doi: 10.1080/0951192X.2013.874589

Chapter 4

Augmented Reality: A Boon for the Teaching and Learning Process

G. Singaravelu

Department of Education, Bharathiar University, Coimbatore, India

Contents

DOI: 10.1201/9781003175896-4

Objectives

This chapter addresses the following objectives:
1. Learn about augmented reality (AR) in education
2. Enrich knowledge on the utilization of AR
3. Comprehend the environment of AR in education
4. Understand the role of AR in the teaching and learning process
5. Equip applications of AR in the classroom
6. Acquire knowledge on future AR in education

4.1 Introduction

Augmented reality (AR) is a platform of a technology (Besin Urologulf, 2020) wherein classroom learning becomes more active and transitional. AR is employed in classrooms all over the world through electronic text and concepts in real social settings employing triggers for learning opportunities. It refers to the use of technology to superimpose information such as images, sounds, and text on the real world. It provides an interactive, reality-based display environment to enrich the real-world experience of users. It advocates and encourages the adoption of real and computer-based scenes and images for teaching learners difficult areas. Audio-video based learning can be enhanced through AR for classroom transactions, and AR simplifies complex learning. AR employs computerized simulation and techniques such as animation, image and speech detection, handheld devices, and powered display environments.

4.2 Augmented Reality

The term "augmented reality" was introduced by Tom Caudell, a former Boeing scientist, in 1990. The idea of enhancement by virtual information was at first employed for various purposes during the late 1960s and 1970s. For the purpose of visualizing and training, AR has been used by many companies since 1990. Schools and universities are using it at present. Personal computers and mobile devices are availed for implementing the concept of AR, especially for replacing traditional educational environments through this innovative teaching and learning mechanism, and exclusively for encouraging classroom transactions between students and teachers and among students. Adding virtual components in AR, such as digital pictures, animations, or sensations, makes AR an innovative form of interaction in the real world. This is the main objective of AR.

4.2.1 Recent Developments and History of AR

Investigators thought AR would improve the knowledge, perceptions, and communication of students. AR has the power to boost productivity in global tasks. However, it was not until the 1990s that inertia became important. AR books are significant stepping stones serving the general public, linking both the digital and physical worlds. AR technology is a good platform to supply students with three-dimensional (3D) shows and asynchronous experiences that are attractive to learners (Figure 4.1).

AR books are often handled at the first stage also. The "Institute of Promoting Teaching Science and Technology in Asian Country created a 3 Dimensional increased reality earth science book that imparts pupils regarding the invention of earth's sheets, their connections, variations, and functions". Magic Book Associate, an AR boundary system, permits students to prepare content in AR for any traditional manuscript, transporting information to life with graphic and co-operative aids drawn from text in the book. "Pupil's area unit is able to use the book, as a result of 3D simulated content connected to [the] book page."

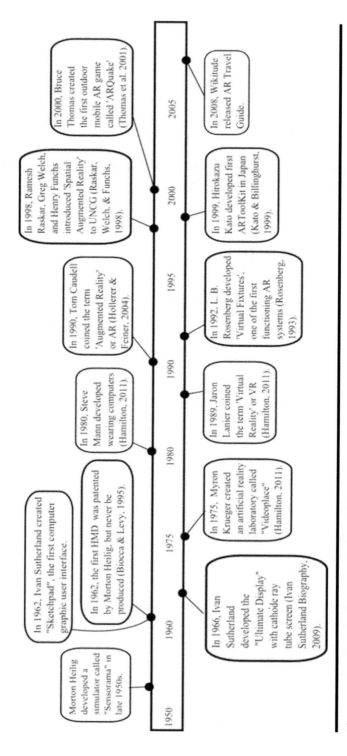

Figure 4.1 History of Augmented Reality – in Brief.

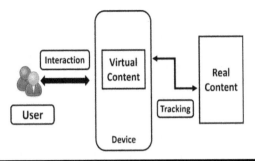

Figure 4.2   Elements of AR System.

Fault-finders of typical writing have started to be aware that videos can be altered. However, AR books are a form of narrating stories to a completely new interface. Readers who are hard to please find the books coherent and excellent. The robustness of AR books is attractive to several types of teaching, using several methods. It will make learning simple and interesting to learners and teachers.

4.2.2 Augmented Reality and Its Elements

AR offers a vision of an original world through devices such as smartphones, tablets, etc. The physical world is shown in real time along with an additional layer of virtual elements. Unlike virtual reality, though, it is not a matter of replacing physical reality, but rather different multimedia elements are placed with the view of the real world: Texts, images, 3D models, videos, audio, and animations. These multimedia elements are stored and associated with a remote server. Hence, it is necessary to have an internet connection on the computer, tablet, or smartphone to retrieve the virtual items and add them to the physical reality. In order to achieve this superposition of virtual elements in the view of the physical environment, an AR system should have the following elements: (Figure 4.2)

> **Camera:** This device captures an image of the real world. It can be a computer webcam or a smartphone or tablet camera.
> **Processor:** This element of hardware combines an image with information that must be superimposed.
> **Software:** This specific computer program manages the process.
> **Screen:** Real and virtual elements are combined on it.
> **Internet connection:** It is used to send information from a real environment to a remote server and recover associated virtual information that overlaps.
> **Activator:** This is a real-world element that software uses to recognize the physical environment and select associated virtual information that is being added. It can be a QR code, a bookmark, an image or object, or a GPS signal to be sent by the device.

Marker: It is an element that is more typical of 3D augmented reality systems. It can be a box printed on paper or an object that we move and place in real space and that the system recognizes and uses as a reference of where to add a virtual 3D model.

4.2.3 Operation of AR Systems

Increased reality is the innovation that grows the material world and comprises more computerized data. Computer-generated reality contrasts AR, which neglects to establish the complete fake conditions to return genuine with the virtual one. The genuine climate is changed by PC-made articles in various fields. Applications are accessible to work advanced liveliness with the assistance of GPS.

Four types of augmented reality:

1. **Markerless Augmented Reality**
   Markerless AR alludes to a product application that is not needed past information on a client's current circumstance to overlay virtual 3D substance into a scene and hold it to a fixed point in space.
2. **Mark-based Augmented Reality**
   This AR application appraises the direction and position of the camera for the casing of the genuine world. As such, most applications utilize marker-based AR.
3. **Projection-based Augmented Reality**
   This AR is also called spatial AR a technique for conveying advanced data inside a fixed setting. Target clients and items can move around in the area; yet, the territory wherein AR is used is restricted to the fields taking into account the fixed projector and supporting camera.
4. **Superimposition-based Augmented Reality**
   Superimposition-based AR is the substitution of items from the real world. This AR generally happens with the partial or whole substitution of the virtual perspective of an item with an expanded view.

4.2.4 Operation of Augmented Reality Framework

AR normally uses data that is gathered from the real world. In the vision field of AR, an item from the virtual area is made by a PC that can broaden the scene from the real world. The AR framework can likewise hold the sensation from the real world. AR alludes to a PC adjusting real data. Representation for utilization of reality incorporates superimposition of interior data over an outside framework. The age of augmented and virtual spaces requires the alliance of space maps related with actual space, which is intermixed into electronic space by the PC (Figure 4.3). Sensor inputs are needed to gather data for the PC, and they are used to introduce

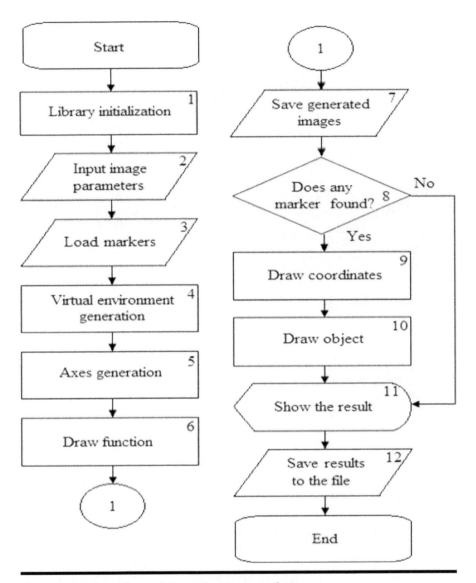

Figure 4.3   Flow Chart of Operating System of AR.

a reflections cycle and to introduce an appearance in the electronic space. The virtual work of the PC is shown sooner or laterFigure 4.3.

4.3 Augmented Reality in Education

Students can learn their lessons via videos, images, and animations by adopting AR in education. AR has captured the attention of students across the country to achieve

Figure 4.4   AR in the Classroom.

academic levels with increased knowledge and a higher rate of retention. Changing the place and timing of learning material is the potential of AR, which can introduce new ways and methods. Classes, through AR, will be more engaging and informative so that students can comprehend concepts. The spokespeople for education are aware of the fact that the learning process includes interaction and creativity.

Most learners have their own smartphones and are active smartphone users. So, smartphones can be used as a device of gameplay and for social interaction with kith and kin. Currently, a large number of students are using mobile devices for educational purposes, such as doing homework assignments, accessing subject-oriented matters, etc. The amalgamation of both phone and AR, especially for educational purposes, isl really popular, although still, it should be exploited further to get the maximum benefit out of it. AR enables students to obtain ample information easily. Now, AR satisfies the needs of learners related to subjects. Of late, the power to link reality and digital content is being enhanced gradually, and enough opportunities are provided for learners and teachers as different technologies are introduced.

"AR can be used in multiple devices (Pc's, tablets, smartphones, wearable components etc.)" (Swensen, 2016), and "it is demarcated in combining virtual and real objects in a real environment through mobile devices, working spontaneously in real-time, showing that there is a combination of virtual and real objects in the same environment" (Azuma et al., 2001) (Figure 4.4).

AR possesses enough power to be employed as an innovative technology in the domain of education. Because of the monotonous style of learning, the quantum of interest and involvement in the classroom of students is getting reduced in modern days, but through technology, teachers can create a healthy learning environment. It encourages learners to obtain knowledge faster. It is often said that technology provides information through digital text, images, animation, and video and audio modes. There are a number of applications developed for students to participate in an interactive learning environment, though AR is in the emerging stage currently. More innovations are needed in the discipline of education.

In the current conventional scenario of education, learning and teaching have become boring. Teachers should think about how students will experience knowledge once they have learned it. Teachers have to think about how this upcoming technology of AR in the classroom will indeed create a system that teachers need to implement virtual reality in education.

4.4 Utilisation of AR in Education

AR Classes help to motivate students, capture their attention as a whole, and help them to understand difficult subjects. Interaction with AR may be part of a lesson like a teaser or it may support the main topic, providing extra information to students. Following are significant utilizations of AR in education and other institutions:

1. **Educational Itineraries**

   AR facilitates and increases the educational use of itineraries for college trips, museums, exhibitions, etc. An added layer can contain text, images, animations, videos, audio, etc., considerably expanding available information. Students can use these already prepared itineraries as a basis for the development of research projects. If the creation tool is affordable, teachers can also develop these AR contents individually and collectively and use them for students. It would increase the possibility of AR in the classroom favoring both consumption and creation of content using this technology.

2. **3D Models**

   There are ideas and processes for measuring the area of a square that are ideal for learning with 3D models and graph paper.

3. **Simulations**

   In the initial phases of learning, the use of AR in simulations allows interesting features such as simplicity, availability, immediacy, safety in practice, trial-and-error learning, cost reduction, etc. For example, in psychology, AR systems are used to treat phobias of patients to spiders and cockroaches. Simulators with AR technology are also used in safety issues such as fire extinguishing, welding with a coated electrode, or cooking a steak.

4. **Real-Time Translators**

   The technology of AR can also be applied to translate existing text into an image in the real world. Word Lens is an application for mobile phones and tablets that captures the image through a camera, recognizes text, translates it into the chosen language, and shows that image on the screen, replacing text with its translation.

5. **Accessibility**

AR can also contribute to increase access to public resources and spaces. This is especially useful for students with educational needs because it increases the possibility of access to information. An example of AR for accessibility is the Accentac Project.

4.4.1 Importance of Augmented Reality

AR has a unique place due to

- Increasing subject understanding
- Learning preparation function
- Learning language institutes
- Retaining long-standing memory
- Improving action performance
- Improving teamwork
- Increasing the inspiration of students
- Experimenting in a more secure environment than handling compounds in real life
- Expanding learning about plants and their interaction with surroundings through virtual expansion cycles
- Saving money that would otherwise restrict students' ability to make observations and investigations in the classroom
- Improving understanding of abstract, spatial geometric notions through exploitation and multi-angle monitoring of digital 3D objects

4.4.2 Advantages of Using AR in Education

The development of the AR application for education has been reworked for the academic division. This paradigm shift has been completed, and it continues to magnify in all areas of the educational domain. Thus, the advantage of AR in education is different because of its remarkable impact. It is understood that AR can still rework education and also the learning method, as below.

1. Increasing students' interest and classroom engagement
2. Practical learning
3. Cheaper cost of learning
4. 24×7 available study materials
5. Growth of memory

4.4.2.1 Nurture Training Method

The utilization of AR in the educational domain creates entertainment and edutainment for college students. The United Nations enhanced their motivation using the AR training method. The reality is that AR instigates higher learning methods in students. It attracts students to the learning track where it becomes important to analyze new concepts. It will increase the inventive art of scholars within the learning method. In the end, students develop ingenuity and the ability to discover and get in touch with additional concepts through this training method.

4.4.2.2 Increasing Students' Participation in Categories

AR will increase the participation of scholars in academic uses through the classroom. With the help of AR apps, pupils possess the possibility of using coaching training models. These models help with high-level acquisition of concepts among scholars. Most pupils will perceive they have a higher understanding of topics through this additional contribution. The often precise results of AR applications in education help scholars understand ideas quicker through the delivered models. In the end, students will have a high level of interest, resulting in dynamic schoolroom participation. Therefore, it will increase the motivation and interest of scholars within the learning method.

4.4.2.3 AR Improving & Increasing Memory

Learners will have training through AR models by scanning, and these models will be informative and have a wider variety of subject matter than other methods. Pupils get access to informative online sites through AR applications engineered by app-creating firms. Such learning expertise develops a strong learning progression for scholars and benefits them to enhance and sustain data across time. It is attainable thanks to the extent of interest that comes with learning through AR. In the end, AR imparts a lofty amount of educational interest and enthusiasm among learners, and it will improve imagination and increase memory power as well.

4.4.2.4 Interactive Lessons by AR

Using AR in the education domain offers asynchronous lessons to pupils. The United Nations possesses complete reachability for informative and asynchronous modules on their learning app. At the end of the day, this offers clear and higher level acquisition of academic ideas and also the best ways to interact with students. It helps in learning and increasing informative activities among students.

4.4.2.5 Increasing Sensory-Motor Development

The utilization of AR in education can support student's physical and psychological development. AR offers the liberty to write and room to carefully listen and perceive concepts at the same time. Therefore, AR offers interactive privileges to assist and better students' physical and psychological faculties. At end of the day, this leads to magnified sensory development and provides an academic learning method to an entirely innovative stage.

4.4.2.6 Less Expensive

The price of academic materials is typically expensive, and the cost of 3D models, posters, and prototypes is not encouraging. Massive complicated academic drawings for faculties are quite pricey. An honest variety of academic centers do not have resources to shop and sustain those materials. The unhappy reality is that a number of such materials get broken and lost; some become exhausted. These learning models need to be available to pupils at home and in the schoolroom. AR minimizes the cost of shopping for learning apparatus and is more cost-effective across a long period as users no longer have to spend money on physical materials.

4.4.2.7 Enriched Ways of Telling a Story

Utilizing AR in the domain of education offers enhanced ways of narrating academic sections via optical models, of which the square measures remain distinctive, and these will facilitate students to check their academic ideas. AR models bring to life academic ideas and methods, and create an impression of originality and realism for educational ideas. AR betters these ideas by giving them an entirely new life, and enriched stories achieve higher academic interactions for college students. These models create a higher and improved understanding of academic ideas.

4.4.2.8 Increasing Learning Activities

Technology has emerged as a necessary element of education, and pupils fully rely upon technology for all things. Interactive models offer access to magnified and enhanced learning activities and enhanced learning interactive activities for college students. AR apps make learning and education pleasing and gratifying for students.

4.4.2.9 Visiting the Past, Present, and Future

AR in education is decisive and encourages scholars to induce data of the past, present, and future. Knowledge regarding academic ideas of exploitation models of all the events that are speculated to use and take students into the past events and identical replicas help in finding out actions in the future for obtaining advantages of combined data to unravel issues within society.

This is often a precise chance offered by utilizing AR in education and enables learners to achieve data of all three events. Therefore, a chance is given to practice data, to undo issues and visit the past, present, and future. Therefore, increased observation and enthusiasm within the learning method are significant roles played by AR.

4.5 AR in Learning and Educational Domain

4.5.1 Five Directions of AR in Educational Environments

4.5.1.1 Discovery-Based Learning

AR can be employed in discovery-based learning, which is offered along with concepts pertaining to real-world situations though simultaneously considering things of concern. This kind of usage is often employed in galleries, planetariums, and ancient places.

4.5.1.2 Objects Modelling

AR may be employed in modelling applications. These types of applications create interest among learners to obtain instant visual feedback by what a particular element will look like in varying settings. Certain applications also allow learners to engineer the virtual objects for analyzing the physical features or communication among objects. This sort of function is also being availed in architectural education.

4.5.1.3 Augmented Reality Books

AR books enable students to use 3D presentations and interactive ways of learning. Books' worth increases with the assistance of technological devices like special glasses. Primary administration of AR books exhibits that this type of mode is probably going to attract learners who are digital natives. It will be used as an instructional medium even at the first level.

4.5.1.4 AR Gaming

Educators choose to use games to help learners with easily understood ideas. Through AR, games are primarily constructed within the real world, and increased networked information will provide effective ways to point out relations and linkages. Marker technology usually represents a flat game that becomes a 3D setting once viewed through mobile device or camera. This sort of game may be applied to a variety of disciplines like anthropology, history, social science, earth science, etc. AR gambling permits players to form simulated people and objects and to bind to particular locations within the universe. Players will act with digital people and objects that appear once the player approaches pertinent coupled locations within the universe.

Present educators have a lot of chances to utilize replacement graphics and collaborative learning through AR. Sims Nails is a collaborative image and teaching aid that helps guests study and test with ideas of common action and development. A recent study discovered a number of prospects in AR gambling for education. As a team, learners in every context had diverse roles and used handheld devices that used GPS technology.

The aim of this sport is to find the reason for aliens coming back to earth and landing in a specific space. Scholars target-hunted to create a hypothesis by grouping proof, and with success, finishing issues. They got to use science, language, and humanities skills. Taking part in the game, scholars interacted with digital virtual characters, digital things, and cluster members to identify a course from a sports house to succeed. "When sport is to carry the eye of a learner, although those bottlenecks are there, it should be kept in mind that AR gambling continues to be in its infancy. As gain a lot of expertise and as design flaws within [the] program area unit pressed out, AR gambling possesses the power to be an efficient device for creating students' interest."

4.5.1.5 Skill Training

AR will spark nearby abilities in an instructive capacity. AR has a strong likelihood to give amazing incidental learning in situational learning experiences and unforeseen examination, however simultaneously, by advancing the connected nature of abstract ideas in the real world.

AR has a solid ability to give amazing logical, situational learning encounters and fortunate investigation while at the same time advancing the revelation of the associated idea of data in reality. AR goggles have effectively prepare peopled, in explicit undertakings, similar to equipment mechanics in the guard and airplane support for Boeing, and furthermore show bit by bit how to fix, distinguish vital devices, and add printed directions.

4.6 Multidisciplinary Use of AR

AR is used in several independent disciplines. Some of them are medicine, designing, diversion, tourism, gaming, and education. Across the world, scholars have used AR to teach language, biology, and foreign languages. Using AR in environmental education increases motivation and encourages self-paced learning. In higher stages, AR includes enhancements over previous methods in terms of engrossment and inspiration. Prendes (2015) says use of AR is appropriate in every academic settings. All those scholars consider that AR is indeed a real tool that will accelerate learning pace to obtain better learning outcomes through pleasant ways and means, and in total it comforts both teachers and students at large.

4.7 Place of AR in Classroom Learning

In teaching and learning platforms, AR as a technology overlays interactive digital parts – like text, pictures, videos, sounds, 3D objects, and computer graphics – into real-world environments. AR improves not only learning but also conjointly offers chances for pupils to form their own opinions. Experts of online technology assist their fellow educators to integrate new technologies. An assortment of online AR tools and programs is available for any subject. The variety of those apps promotes skills like originality, problem solving, crucial thinking, analysis, coding, and pragmatic testing.

Many teachers have attempted to write their own lesson plans. They become fascinated with AR as an educational method, especially for encouraging students to study facts regarding history or science. AR can help students achieve an improved understanding of these topics. Most teachers are ready to walk their students through times and places in history to assist them to do higher thinking because they are experts on these subjects.

AR is accustomed to scanning footage to gather a lot of data or to copy text to acquire messages, facilitate, and assign schoolwork. Scanning a book's jacket might provide students with a brief outline of the book. Certain applications are already available that enable students to scan book covers and transfer reviews regarding them.

In modern times, the following are practiced in the process of teaching and learning in the classroom.

1. AR-Enabled Worksheets

This helps students to experience AR technology from their homes. The tedious process of homework can be converted into an easy one for students, and they can explore both AR and content at their homes. These worksheets will enable students to construct positive relationship between technology and education.

2. Faculty Photo Walls

Creating a faculty photo wall in classrooms is a creative method to integrate AR in education. This wall has pictures of faculty members on a display board. Using AR, students or visitors can scan images for their future reference. This is out-of-the-box thinking, which enables learning more information about teachers and getting all possible information. A word wall is another concept in which learners can see meanings and drawings of key vocabulary words by using AR-based word walls in a collaborative environment. It will help students to improve their vocabularies. Students can make use of their mobile devices to learn usages of words and sentences.

AR can also be used for parent involvement. It helps parents to keep track of regular activities being held at institutions. Augmented trigger images from parents can be attached at each student's desk to boost their confidence through a few words of motivation.

3. Custom-Made Markers

Marker images serve the purpose of displaying AR content over a surface. For this, AR must be directly linked to lesson content. Learners can point their camera towards AR textbook pages, and the AR application identifies it and sends a query to the server immediately. The camera pointed at the page fiducially serves like a registrating device for orientation and movement of an image that allows an object to rotate at all angles. This is implemented today in a wide array of applications in education. Aurasma and Layar are two applications that use this program, which can be set up easily.

Through this, teachers can trigger "Aura" to an online matter that can be in the form of video, internet content, or a non-dynamic image. When viewers check over Aura, they are provided online content in a floating window that proves to be highly engaging for students.

4. Premade Resources

This is one of the easiest implementations of AR technology in classrooms. This kind of content helps teachers take away the stress of getting involved in the technological phase of lesson planning. But this, again, provides learners with a means to carry on with the subject. It is a good platform to start for teachers. It is a very good intuitive process for students, and all they need is a smartphone to bring pages of a textbook to life. Several mobile companies are now coming with textbooks with AR possibilities encoded. Carlton Books is a leading international publisher that publishes beautifully illustrated books for both adults and children. It creates AR books that bring each and every page of a book to life. They specialize in popular topics such as arts, lifestyle, entertainment, history, puzzles, etc.

4.8 Experiences of AR in the Classroom

For using AR in training, we will acknowledge useful models for classrooms all throughout the world. According to Giasiranis and Sofos (2017) in "Portrayal of Information in PC" the work of AR has an additional value in bringing in training and contributing with more constructive outcomes inside the scope of educating and learning measures. The work of AR inside the schoolroom makes instructive techniques extra successful, dynamic, and huge. It is more intriguing for analysts, and it is all-around acknowledged by clients. Students of the United Nations comprehend the

Figure 4.5   AR in the Classroom.

benefits of its utilization in education. The UN office said it has effectively no heritable abilities in advances that urge them to utilize the previous system. Whereas in elective cases, the work of AR and antiquated systems didn't show variety for Tosik Gun and Atasoy (2017), in the sixth subject of "Mathematical Items Associate in a Volume of Estimation" utilizing the style of partial-test study that looks at data acquired by one group and a trial group, during which the specialists utilized real objects for the first case and AR for the second case (Figure 4.5).

Its utilization in teaching chemistry in classrooms has been dissected and it improves comprehension of chemistry outcomes. In conclusion, AR is coordinated in a positive way in educating and contributes to the improvement of evaluations. Subsequently, these models show AR is being incorporated into classrooms throughout the world.

4.8.1 AR Technology in the Classroom

The learning process can be made fruitful by using AR technology in classroom transactions. 3D figures are easier for students to comprehend. AR can be used to assure the effectiveness of the classroom as follows:

1. **Abstract and Complex Topics:** Abstract and complex items taught through traditional methods are challenging, but they can be simplified by using AR in the classroom.
2. **Experiment with Stimulation:** AR technology provides 3D stimulation, through which students are able to get hands-on training in all experiments, which is easier and more cost-effective than an actual laboratory.
3. **Kindle the Passion of Learning:** AR can kindle the passion of students in learning, which creates interest and brings effective outcomes in learning.

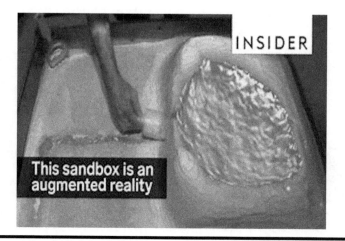

Figure 4.6 AR in the Classroom.

4. **Making Classes Interactive:** AR is an interactive technology, and it is based on a learner-centered approach.
5. **Improving Collaboration and Co-operation:** By using AR, the teacher is a facilitator and coordinator instead of a manager of the class.

4.8.2 Augmented Reality Tools for the Science Classroom

Energy Quest, a brand-new title from CPO Science Link, is an innovative and useful addition to the natural science program. For using AR and gameplay, the student is ready to act with ideas of metastasis and photosynthesis – topics that are generally powerful for college students to know. The Energy Quest program incorporates varying levels and details in every game, and AR activity permits teachers to customize academic expertise to match students' needs and understanding. AR components conjointly permit students to act with a 3D cell, providing a brand-new perspective and additional comprehensive and interactive visual expertise.

4.8.3 Augmented Reality in the Classroom

There are five ways to use AR in the classroom:

1. Aurasma: Teacher brings AR into the classroom by creating their own experience.
2. Daqri Studio: It is an option for teachers to design their own AR experiences.
3. Quiver: It is used for coloring pages for every subject area (Figure 4.6).
4. Fetch Lunch Rush: This is a free game to use printable cards as AR pieces.
5. Aug That: Animated lessons come in a variety of formats through 3D and 360-degree views.

4.9 Place of Augmented Reality in Teaching

AR should modify the very foundations of education, irreversibly modernizing it and absolutely perceiving categories to assess and interact with scholars. Teachers perceive that education must be more than simply reading and being attentive to lectures. It conjointly must involve interaction and creativeness. To make learning pleasant to learners and make sure that they keep involved, those students have to be engaged, and AR may be a good thing to try. Teachers try to find ways to assist their students to learn quicker and retain more information. AR technology could permit teachers to provide advantages to students that may prove priceless to them for the remainder of their lives.

AR technology is an unaccustomed sphere of education. The potential for brand new teaching strategies and the advantages to the teaching sphere are unbelievable. Creativity in teaching and learning are right around the corner, as educators get access to AR tools. Teachers' classrooms are modified; however, progress towards additional participating lessons and enhanced learning will probably take longer to implement.

4.9.1 Technology and Youth Culture

Children of the modern age have smartphones and tablets. They use them for searching the internet, watching videos, and participating in chats with friends. These are good resources for locating information that may help them augment their learning outcomes. Youths of today love technology and employ it in their daily lives. Therefore, why not take a brand new and interesting technology and use it to draw their attention and embark on the learning process like never before? Education will be more engaging, and students can interact in a fresh way through which they can inculcate the passion of learning.

4.9.2 AR Makes Troublesome Ideas Easier to Understand

In discrimination AR technology, 3D models will be developed on any content. Teachers will take terribly abstract or complicated ideas and make them tangible for college students. Scholars will approach different matters and have an additional concrete understanding of how to make them available for visual learners. AR technology is employed for producing support to oral presentations and traditional teaching-learning materials. In short, AR-enabled technology will help students to learn difficult ideas in simple and diversified ways.

4.9.3 Interactions and Involvement

Obtaining all students' attention for every assignment and lesson may be a cumbersome task that teachers experience on a daily basis. Some students are reluctant to be told

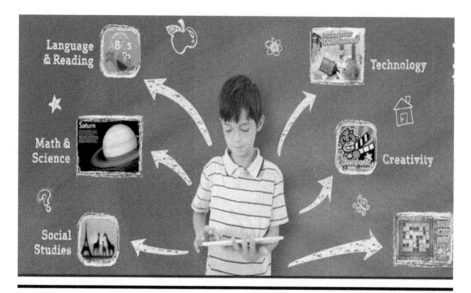

Figure 4.7 Pedagogical Subjects in AR.

alternatives and do not interact with fellow students. They will be brought out of their seclusion and encouraged to participate through the utilization of 3D models and AR interaction. This innovative technology will capture their attention. AR interaction will be considered to be a precursor to a bigger lesson, piquing students' interest and making certain that they are listening to remember the lesson.

4.9.4 Pedagogical Skills

AR may also be used to teach students specific real-world skills that they could not gain in a typical classroom. They will be placed in safe surroundings and learn the way to control machinery, perform tasks, and develop skills in the classroom (Figure 4.7).

They will steel themselves for their chosen profession with priceless coaching created by trade specialists. Students now need not be passive observers. However, they will move and become engaged with content. This could build training methods to create expertise and make sure that the information they gain sticks with them.

4.10 Impact of AR

The main advantage of using AR within the education sector is that it fully modifies the way teachers use books and obtain knowledge. AR exhibits subject matter within 3D videos, images, graphics, etc. Beyond any doubt, it will increase student's interaction and attendance in the classroom. Students can learn at any point in time, from any place, by the assistance of AR applications on smartphones. This technique is certainly useful for teaching methods that students like to use. It sufficiently receives number one position among foremost important trends in education.

In a nutshell, a variety of AR implementation measures are obtainable on mobile phones within classrooms. Several e-learning development corporations conjointly leverage the ability of AR in their e-learning platforms. At work, AR will produce entirely new learning experiences, or just supplement current coaching initiatives. Written learning materials will be delivered by taking one thing stationary and infusing it with animation and interactivity that engages the learner and demonstrates views that cannot be shown with one static thing. Group activities will be reworked into interactive treasure hunts that get learners up and moving as they scan things to unravel clues and procure new information on methods.

4.11 Using AR for Learning and Development

The following AR tools are used for learning enhancement in the domain of education:

- 3DBear
- Catchy Words AR
- Co Spaces Edu
- Froggipedia
- Jig Space
- MERGE Cube
- Metaverse
- Moat boat
- Orb

4.11.1 Best AR Applications and Resources in Classrooms

Options for AR use are endless, and many AR apps and resources are employed in classrooms to produce subject matter and communication for college pupils, as below:

- **Popular Toys:** This catalog of AR has the potential to modify scanned books, scrutinize posters or complete puzzles, and get pleasure from interactive books on planets, bugs, dinosaurs, safari, and ocean life or maybe interactive charts on human anatomy, periodic tables, world maps, etc.
- **Daqri:** It is one among towering reality developers. Daqri is the creator of Daqri Studio – an artistic tool for planning your own AR for science. You can cross-check anatomy in 4D.
- **Quiver or Colar App:** This has various coloring texts in each field. Once associated with the app, coloring pages return to life with animated actions. As an example, learners will produce their own flag to fly, tie it to science, and fly it in the dominant wind.

- **Chromville:** It is based on coloring pages of science that kindle ability in kids through art and technology under eight multiple intelligences. The visual app characters are used to market storytelling, and the optional schoolroom part has coloring pages.
- **Fetch Lunch Rush:** This game application is fun and uses printable cards as an AR game. Within this game app, children help Ruff Dog feed dish to a picture show crew by resolving math issues. Every game piece can be an active image that comes to life once scanned.
- **STAR - AR Worksheets:** In this interactive material, the worksheet comes alive and transposes 3D models and video resources to strengthen the content.

4.11.2 Augmented Reality Applications for Classroom

	HP Reveal The idea of high-power unit Reveal (previously "Aurasma") is a simple one. Teachers will build any image (an icon, graphics, text document,) scan it, and make it ready with a mobile device (iOS or Android), with associated action. The associated action will be a film show, an additional clarification show, advice from an internet site, etc.
	CoSpacesedu This app is meant for the creation of content through an app for learners. Co Spaces can help pupils create their own 3D objects. Learners exploit their talents to come with creations. It allows learners to project their creations in real-world AR. Students create using their hands with MERGE Cube.
	Wonder scope is an app that narrates stories. This app uses AR to redesign the normal idea into period stories. Students learn together to scan with the app. Students can raise inquiries to characters within the story and hear answers.
	Layar This reality software system, enhance learner fliers, postcards, and items with collaborative content, as well as MMS, internet and social media, image slides, audio clips, and a lot more.
	Shapes 3D This AR application is for scientific disciplines or to show pure mathematics. It begins with simple straightforward images and bit by bit explores the most complicated ones. This AR device reinforces teachers' ability and supplies prospects to point out concepts that cannot be shown with physical tools.

	Google Expeditions It provides a combination between AR and VR and permits a coach to help learners through 360° scenes, 3D models, saying attention-grabbing links, and artefact means. They need several AR courses. Learners will download free apps and discover science, history, arts, and nature. It is accessible for IiOS and Android.
	Metaverse Students will enjoy games in AR, go geo-caching, build puzzles, select their own journey, and go on scavenger hunts. With this studio, academics will produce their own interactive stories and jailbreak games for college students.
	SnapChat Believe it or not, nearly each SnapChat filter relies on AR technology. Academics will put filters on footage and shape them to stand out. Learners can even build AR filters on their own.
	Google Translate This application is employed to translate words on objects, and learners will have the ability to translate text.
	AR Makr AR Makr may be an inventive chest for AR. Using this app, pupils will sketch, scan, and snap the surroundings they encounter. It allows them to rework creations from 2D to 3D virtual objects. Once a coach will produce a 3D AR object, the teacher will place his/her creations anyplace in his/her surroundings. Learners even record scenes, and save and share them with their teacher.
	Book Review Learners will merely record a video on their own explaining a book. Academics will build one long video. Students will build drawings that say one thing concerning every chapter. Then, they will record a video to clarify drawings.
	Interactive wall It can build videos of solutions for a giant instructional question. It can use footage to make virtual videos. On the first day, students and their parents will scan photographs.
	Discover world This is to earn points by participating in games that have been created by a mentor. As an example, if a coach needs to show Egypt, the teacher will build a computer game using this application.

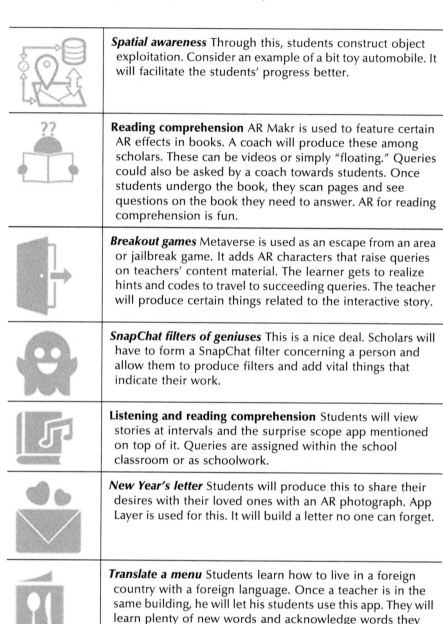

Spatial awareness Through this, students construct object exploitation. Consider an example of a bit toy automobile. It will facilitate the students' progress better.

Reading comprehension AR Makr is used to feature certain AR effects in books. A coach will produce these among scholars. These can be videos or simply "floating." Queries could also be asked by a coach towards students. Once students undergo the book, they scan pages and see questions on the book they need to answer. AR for reading comprehension is fun.

Breakout games Metaverse is used as an escape from an area or jailbreak game. It adds AR characters that raise queries on teachers' content material. The learner gets to realize hints and codes to travel to succeeding queries. The teacher will produce certain things related to the interactive story.

SnapChat filters of geniuses This is a nice deal. Scholars will have to form a SnapChat filter concerning a person and allow them to produce filters and add vital things that indicate their work.

Listening and reading comprehension Students will view stories at intervals and the surprise scope app mentioned on top of it. Queries are assigned within the school classroom or as schoolwork.

New Year's letter Students will produce this to share their desires with their loved ones with an AR photograph. App Layer is used for this. It will build a letter no one can forget.

Translate a menu Students learn how to live in a foreign country with a foreign language. Once a teacher is in the same building, he will let his students use this app. They will learn plenty of new words and acknowledge words they already learned.

Aurasma: This app permits users to interact and have AR experiences. Students will utilize this app to convert their learning to real life. Aurasma is often employed in alternative ways in the classroom.

PreparationMini-Lessons: Students scan a page of their work, which reveals the video of the teacher trying to solve the puzzle.

School Picture Wall: Through this college, photos close to the college entrance will be discovered. Guests will scan any picture and see it come to life, narrating things important to students.

Book Reviews: Learners record themselves giving a quick review of something special that they finished, thus join that "air" to a book. Thereafter, anybody can examine the sofa-bed of the book and right away access the survey.

Yearbooks: From accolades for video profiles, from sports features to productions and show film, manners by which AR will improve a yearbook are boundless.

Lab Safety: Place triggers (pictures that enact media once checked by a gadget) all-around a working environment. Students will rapidly learn different well-being strategies and conventions for research facility instrumentality.

Hard of Hearing and Difficult of Hearing (dhh) Language Cheat Sheets: With AR, cheat sheets of jargon words will contain a video overlay that gives an approach to a word or expression.

World Simulations with Interactive Objects: These simulations are integrally immersive once done properly. However, the app will create a lot of work by adding clickable objects and hot spots.

Insecure eLearning Situations in Real-time: AR could be a robust and life-saving device. Doctors will apply advanced processes while not endangering their patients. Additionally, mechanized operators have the flexibility to comfortably steer their tools in an exceedingly safe atmosphere. Nearly any trade that is risky will enjoy AR situations. Best of all, it often occurs in real time so that workers experience similar pressure and stress. It mimics each side of the world's state of affairs. As a result, workers gain valuable expertise, minus geographical point injuries. Each call they create ends up with a unique outcome and permits them to envision the implications of their actions.

Immersive Stories: AR stories is one among foremost emotion-oriented devices. e-Learning personnel will weave stories that draw online learners in and create comfort with e-learning characters. Simply imagine ballooning those emotions by putting online learners into a major role. AR books are for new readers in fictional environments.

AR Resource Links that Feature Facts and Stats: Individuals will scan a unique AR code or trigger object to be told questions. For instance, a science textbook would possibly take readers to a virtual laboratory wherever they do experiments. It may include AR resource links into e-Learning materials. These will disclose fascinating facts, statistics, and concepts that enable them to explore on their own.

Three-Dimensional Learning Models: This is the foremost advanced uses of AR in e-Learning with 3D and demos. Earlier online learners would read still pictures, figures, and maps on their monitor. AR activities provide flexibility to govern 3D visualizations in order to read it from each side and even move with hot spots to be told a lot of concerning individual parts. For instance, a clickable 3D diagram of producing instrumentality throws lights on key options and functions of every half. AR users can familiarize themselves with machinery and how to use it correctly. These rules are often employed in any difficult way. For instance, a model that demonstrates chemical change at a cellular level.

On-line Group Collaboration Projects that Span the World: e-Learning AR is not only for interactive usages. Indeed, it permits online students from the world to move with their fellow learners in virtual settings. It possesses two efficient uses in online coaching. One is that workers will attend a live company e-Learning incident that options increased live activities with live social settings. This stops hurdles and keeps totally immersed within online deliberation. Another use is online group collaboration. Earth science is not an impairment, as online learners have the ability to exchange concepts and feedback in an exceedingly online discussion point. The students are capable of using cell phones and smart glasses to create expertise, even a lot of interaction.

4.12 Future Augmented Reality in Education

Learning procedure is influenced by AR and its power to modify placement and time of analysis. The new and extra ways and ability of AR technology will build courses. Educators perceive that educational procedures ought to be concerned with imagination and interaction. Their objective is to urge students to be inquisitive about a subject, whereas academics do not have to amuse students with arithmetic.

It has been approved that fast dynamic features of modern information technologies are radically changing things for academics and teaching.

Tools facilitating AR are yet to emerge. AR in education has a tendency to use easy AR in education at intervals every three years across U.S campuses. AR possesses unquestionable areas where it has had a good impact on education. Various fields have already shown potential to gain sweeping enhancements.

A similar prediction holds true for less complicated AR employed by academic actions, considered and enforced by the smaller groups, driven especially by less-financed educators. Teachers demonstrate with AR devices, making unique routines and ways of imparting, communicating, and helping learners' exploration. Through this, a steady and constant improvement is formed.

Consistent with Dede (2008), involvement of this kind, attainable through AR instructional activities, is crucial. Twenty-first century education equips students to face the problems of the current dynamic and technology-oriented world.

For instance, students need to learn how to solve issues as a group, to plan to confront any test in their future careers that AR will answer, possibly conceptualized by individuals acting alone. Likewise Dede (2008) brings up "those popular students had the chance to figure out how 'to discover' and 'characterize' issues before the revelation of settling" the matter. A great deal of consciousness of self, of others, of things, conditions, feasible prospects, results, and impacts of AR is required. Popular students ought to get abilities identified with self-guided and group reflection for sure, to arrive at obstacles that they will confront. Teachers could become tougher, and students ought to be better at predicting cutting edge reality.

Dede (2008) calls attention to fundamental capacities for contemporary substitutes, such as making and creating unpretentious reproductions, portrayals, and gadgets, and recognizing designs and genuinely human movement. The UN office sees remarkable perspectives that substitutes ought to pick estimations of different perspectives. Predictable with Dede (2008), "abilities will be productively gotten by clients by teaming up with intelligent and vivid Augmented Reality and Virtual Reality instructional exercises. Through figuring out how to receive virtual personas, though teaming up in virtual undertakings, issues, and games, students will part themselves from antagonistic self-originations and squares that may some way or another obstruct their learning."

Dede (2008) states "vivid encounters, especially those inside the clients carry on shifts in character will encourage popular students to achieve bigger awareness of different perspectives. In addition, through set learning contained AR and VR disadvantage discovering games and activities, students show intensified ability to move what they 'know' into entirely unexpected things both in AR and VR. Expanded Reality has numerous applications in different areas, however without a doubt, its utilization in instruction and preparing is something that offers numerous prospects. Association level to subject becomes inside and out, wherein understudy will take a gander at data and examination direct as though actually accessible in the homeroom". These separated, designing, and clinical establishments require all the more constant useful preparing. With the progression in innovation of AR applications, preparing and learning become simple, compelling, and productive. This AR innovation will be a shelter for all clients, particularly teachers as children in general gain from their tablets and cell phones with admittance to the web in a calm, lovely way.

References

Azuma, R. (1997). A survey of augmented reality. *Presence: Teleoperators and Virtual Environments*, 6(4), 355–385. Retrieved from http://www.cs.unc.edu/~azuma/ARpresence.pdf

Azuma, R., Baillot, Y., Behringer, R., Feiner, S., Julier, S., & MacIntyre, B. (2001). Recent advances in augmented reality, *Computers & Graphics*, 21(6), 1–15.

Augmentedrealityon.com. Archived from original on 5 April 2012. Retrieved 18 June 2019.

Billinghurst, M. (2002). Augmented reality in education. *New Horizons for Learning*, December 2002. Retrieved July 20, 2010 from http://www.newhorizons.org/strategies/Technology/billinghurst.htm

Billinghurst, M., & Kato, H. (2002). Collaborative augmented reality. *Communications of ACM*, 45(7), 64–70.

Billinghurist, M. (2013). *Augmented reality in education, teaching and learning strategies.* http://www.newhorizons.org

Cheng, K. H., & Tsai, C. C. (2013). Affordances of augmented reality in science learning suggestions for future research. *Journal of Science Education and Technology*. https://www.scirp.org/(S(351jmbntvnsjt1aadkposzje))/reference/

Dede, C. (2008). Immersive interfaces for engagement and learning. *Science*, *323*, 66–368. doi: 10.1126/science.1167311

De Lorenzo, R. (2009). Augmented reality and on-demand learning. *Mobile Learner*. Retrieved July 22, 2010 from http://mobilelearner.wordpress.com/2009/10/17/augmented-reality-and-on-demand-learning

Dennis, W. (2016). Lengthy History of Augmented Reality. Huffington Post.

Dunleavy, M, & Dede, C. (2013). Augmented Reality Teaching and Learning, In. J. Michael Spector, M. David Merrill, J. Elen, & M. J. Bishop (Eds.).Handbook of Research on Educational Communications and Technology (pp. 735–745). New York: Springer. 10.1007/978-1-4614-3185-5_59.

Giasiranis, S., & Sofos, L. (2017). Flow experience and educational effectiveness of teaching informatics using AR, *Educational Technology & Society*, 20(4), 78–88.

Huang, Y., Li, H., & Fong, R. (2015). Using augmented reality in early art education: A case study in Hong Kong kindergarten. *Early Child Development and Care*, 186(6), 1–16. doi: .10.1080/03004430.2015.1067888.

Schmalstieg, D. (2001). An introduction to augmented reality [PowerPoint slides]. Retrieved from Lecture Notes Online Web site: http://www.iswc.ethz.ch/events/tutorials/slides_schmalstieg.pdf.

Tosik Gün, E., & Atasoy, B. (2017). The effects of augmented reality on elementary school students' spatial ability and academic achievement. *Education and Science*, *42*(191), 31–51.10.15390/eb.2017.7140.

https://elearning.easygenerator.com, Data accessed 30 Sep 2021

https://elearningindustry.com, Data accessed 30 Sep 2021

https://github.com/sunneach/SlideBlast, Data accessed 30 Sep 2021

https://inaugment.com/augmented_reality_in_education, Data accessed 30 Sep 2021

https://mafiadoc.com, Data accessed 30 Sep 2021

https://newatlas.com/chromville-augmented-reality-coloring/32924, Data accessed 1 Oct 2021

https://thinkmobiles.com/blog/augmented-reality-real-estate, Data accessed 1 Oct 2021

https://www.bookwidgets.com/blog/2018/12/10-fun-augmented-reality-apps, Data accessed 1 Oct 2021

https://www.digitaltrends.com/mobile/best-augmented-reality-apps, Data accessed 1 Oct 2021

https://www.newgenapps.com/blog/augmented-reality-apps-ar-examples-succ, Data accessed 1 Oct 2021

Chapter 5

New Horizons for Learning: Augmented Reality in Education

P. Janardhana Kumar Reddy

Associate Professor, Department of Education, Bharathiar University, Coimbatore, India

Contents

DOI: 10.1201/9781003175896-5

Objectives

This chapter addresses the following objectives:

1. Effectively instill required knowledge and skills in students by adopting and integrating new technology in the teaching-learning process
2. Clarify the features of augmented reality (AR) in education in the teaching and learning process
3. Find out the use of open instructive resources in teaching and learning
4. Discover and use of virtual reality and AR in teaching and learning
5. Look at the benefits, challenges, and issues of AR in education in teaching and learning activities

---

5.1 Introduction

In present times, the utilization of innovation to propel education and learning encounters in classrooms has advanced. To that extent, we realize no study has measured how the kind of substance – static or dynamic – can influence the student's learning of information in the augmented reality (AR) application. To choose what the kind of substance means for the learning practice of the student, a test plan in which the student cooperates with the application, utilizing static and dynamic substances, for learning points associated with an electronic foundations course was performed.

One feature about the practice of AR is the addition and communication between the virtual and real allows enormous adaptability and originality in an application. AR can be helpful in more than a few studies and learning parts and represents an important value in that it insists on a mere practical and new interface. Like life science courses, it also is likely to trigger content that combines other environments, in the classroom as well as in any learning surroundings. Therefore, AR permits the expansion of subjects in which every person can have access in different situations. And, consequently, it boosts the interface amid scrutiny of real life and adds descriptive and hypothetical subjects (like Eco MOBILE).

This elasticity, accessible by the tools of AR, permits developed research and investigation of the real, by the prelude of simulated explanations. In reality, when exposed to a real situation, AR subjects allow learners to understand more through the developed flexibility made in real time.

5.2 Augmented Reality

AR is a collaborating occurrence to a real-life situation where substances that are a feature of real life are improved by virtual data, occasionally through numerous sensual modalities – optical, aural, haptic, somatosensory, and olfactory.

This knowledge is naturally linked to the physical world; like that, it has a deep aspect of the existent circumstances. In this technique, AR varies one's continuing insight of the real-life atmosphere, while cyber realities totally restore the handler's real-life atmosphere with a replicated one. AR is linked mainly with two identical footings like mixed reality and computer-mediated reality.

The most imperative significance of AR is how the tool of the numerical world merges into an individual's interpretation of real life, not like an easy show of information, but throughout the adding together of the immerse sensations, as a natural part of an atmosphere.

AR allows you to get your hands on a better ordinary environment or circumstances and receive a perceptually enriched experience. With the help of higher AR technologies, information about the nearby real life of the user becomes collaborative and numerically works. Information about the atmosphere, its bits and pieces, is overlaid on the accurate sphere.

These data, either virtual or real, give information like electromagnetic waves overlaid in the correct position where they lie in space. AR has got a lot of possibilities in the assembly and distribution of unspoken facts. Very deep information combines with additional information like score over the live video feed of an important occasion. AR technology and heads-up display (HUD) are merged together (Figure 5.1).

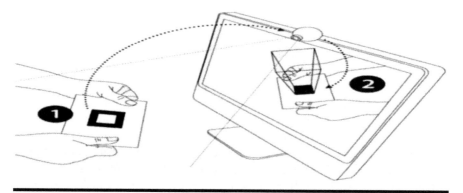

Figure 5.1 The Process of the Augmented Reality Appearance (Billing Hurst, M., 2002).

5.2.1 Importance of Augmented Reality

Technology has transformed into a fundamental piece of our lives. It has changed how individuals reflect and relate to information. One of the most recent innovations is AR, which can be applied to PCs, tablets, and cell phones.

AR bears the cost of the inclination to cover pictures, text, video, and sound segments on top of open pictures. AR innovation gains in the instructive commercial center for its ability to interface the hole and bring a more accessible methodology towards training. Student-focused learning is improved by the reconciliation of virtual and certifiable encounters.

AR overlays imaginary objects or information onto physical objects/environments, resulting in an assorted reality in which imaginary objects and genuine surroundings mutually exist in a significant way for an AR learning experience. AR and virtual reality (VR) use the same technology (hardware) and use plenty of factors similar to computer-generated virtual scenes, objects with 3D, and inter-activity.

AR supports teachers to use digital content with a set of information along with the geographic location of the object/place. Digital information displays on the monitor when teachers scan any object/place using their mobile device with AR technology. Due to the rapid growth in mobile technology, now it is possible to use AR technology in learning (Qualcomm technologies, 2018; Tanya, 2020). The recent growth in mobile devices makes it possible for mobile AR technology to hold up outside learning, which is improved through computer simulation and virtual things with a focus on real situations (Figure 5.2).

AR knows how to be functional in a different playing field of education, starting from kindergarten in primary school to different post-graduate studies. With the use of AR, one can visualize places that can't be explored in real life. For example, mathematical formulas are difficult to visualize as stated.

AR refers to an interactive experience in which technology infuses digital information into a user's insight of the actual world. Access to this world can be

Figure 5.2 The Important Difference between Virtual Reality and Augmented Reality.

via head-mounted or handheld equipment designed specifically for AR, or through a computer monitor, special eyeglasses, gaming devices, or even a smartphone. A simple example of AR might be the projection of numerical data via Google Glass to inform a surgeon of a patient's vital signs during a procedure.

5.3 Directions of AR in Academic Environments

The Five Directions by Yuen et al. to implement AR in the academic sector are as follows.

5.3.1 Discovery-Based Learning

AR will be employed in real situations that alter discovery primarily based on learning. Any user can be supplied with data in a couple of real-world places while at the same time considering something of interest.

5.3.2 Objects Modeling

AR may be used in Objects Modeling applications. Such applications welcome students to require delivery of direct visual recommendations on a given item, which appears in a very large setting. Some apps additionally let learners style virtual objects to look at their communications between objects.

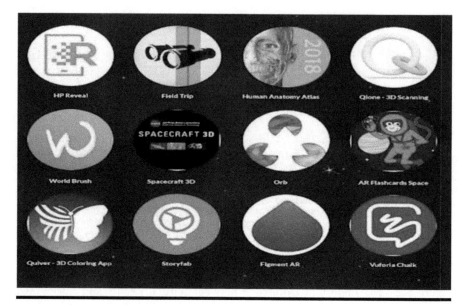

Figure 5.3   Augmented Reality Apps.

5.3.3 Augmented Reality Books

AR Books are unit books that supply student's with a 3D presentation and experiences in interactive learning with AR technology. These books are supplemented with the assistance of 3D glasses. The primary use of AR Books shows that the app is probably used for digital learners, which makes it an applicable academic medium even at the beginner level (Figure 5.3).

5.3.4 Skills Coaching

The support of coaches in specific tasks is represented by skills coaching. Particularly mechanical skill areas can be supported by AR applications. Such presentations are, for example, employed in plane maintenance. Every step of a repair is displayed, necessary tools are shown, and directions are enclosed. The applications are typically used with a head-mounted display (HMD).

5.3.5 Augmented Reality Gaming

Video games supply important new opportunities for learners that were unavailable several years ago. At present, students have found and sometimes utilize games in academic areas. AR allows games that manifest in the virtual world and use increased virtual data. AR games offer learners new ways to connect and make relationships. In addition, they supply learners with cooperative and visual learning.

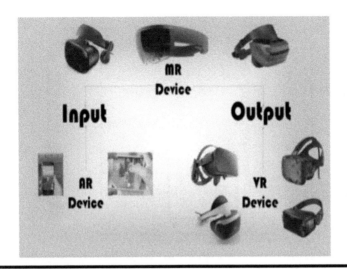

Figure 5.4 AR Technology Tools.

5.4 Technologies for Augmented Reality

AR and computer games use identical hardware technology and share many factors like virtual scenes generated by the computer, 3D objects, and interactivity (Figure 5.4).

The biggest distinction is where the computer game aims to intersect the real world whereas AR, with all respect, enhances it. The first components for AR are devices; input (PCs, chase devices, and monitor-based devices) and output (HMDs) are two vital styles of screens employed in AR, both pictures and optical systems.

5.4.1 Hardware

Hardware elements in AR are sensors, processors, displays, and input devices. Popular mobile devices like Android phones and tablets contain these components, which frequently embrace the camera and sensors like a measuring system, global positioning system, and reliable compass, making them appropriate AR devices. There is technology employed in AR: reflective waveguides and diffractive waveguides.

5.4.2 Display

Several technologies are used in AR, including projectors, monitors, handheld devices, and available display systems. An HMD could be a display device worn on the forehead, like a helmet. Fashionable HMDs usually use sensors up to six points of freedom observance, which permits the display to transfer cybernetic data to the real world and alter according to the user's head movements (Figure 5.5).

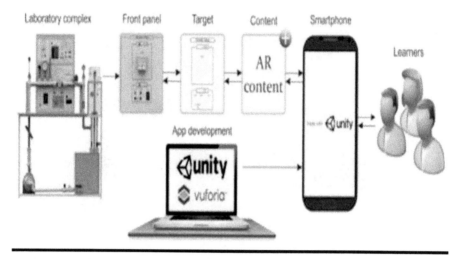

Figure 5.5 Structures of the AR System.

5.4.3 Eyeglasses

AR displays can work like glasses. Some versions employ cameras to increase the view over the eyepieces and accessories. Where the AR representational process is mirrored, the surfaces of the eyeglasses are tainted.

5.4.4 Heads-Up Display or Executive Department

A HUD can be a clear display that presents information while users still see their normal view. A pioneering technology to AR, HUDs were initially designed for pilots (1950), projecting easy flight information into their vision, thus encouraging them to keep their heads up and not to look down at the instrument. Front-eye AR objects may be utilized as transportable HUD to show data and pictures instead of the view of the user.

5.4.5 Contact Lenses

Samsung describes an AN-AR contact, which, once finished, will be a contact lens that contains a camera. The look to regulate its border is a fixed eye blinking. It has to be joined with the user's smartphone to evaluate footage and manage it on an individual basis. It may be something from a lightweight detector to a temperature detector.

5.5 Need and Significance of AR in Education

The introduction of data and information and computer technology (ICT) was not solely in colleges, but conjointly in teaching establishments. It was welcomed by students

Figure 5.6   The Impact of Augmented Reality in Education.

and learners worldwide. Most transmission applications offered for teaching utilize instructional material in a variety of formats, together with text, images, videos, animations, and sound. All these tools typically build on older teaching strategies, creating a topic more attention-grabbing and complex for students and teachers. Accordingly, any future systems and methods should take into account these trends and wishes of the higher education sector that is embracing these new technologies quickly (Figure 5.6).

Many universities are eager to exploit new visualization strategies to boost the current teaching models, and AR is among the foremost promising technologies that presently exist. In technical terms, AR is an associate merger of tricks, vision, and transmission that enhances the user's opinion of the world through cybernetic info. In AR, the important surroundings should be blended with the virtual in place and context to produce an understandable and purposeful read.

5.6 National Education Policy 2019 and Implementation of AR

5.6.1 Technology Use and Integration in Instructional Settings

The New Education Policy 2019 (draft) conjointly emphasized the importance of ICT, AR, and video games in education and recommended to implement an equivalent teaching-learning method for the approaching school year at the education level.

Technology use and incorporation are going to be pursued as a very significant plan for raising the general quality of education. Therefore, the main target won't simply air making and delivering prime excellence content, however conjointly, on

Figure 5.7 Augmented Reality in Education and Training.

pursuit technology to support the translation of content into manifold languages, help learners with special needs, and improve the standard of pedagogy and learning processes through the use of smart tutoring systems and adaptive assessment systems.

Technology use will generate new interactive and immerse content to strengthen instructional design and management, and to bring clarity and potency to the assessment method as well as to the body and authority process to assist with the management of education like subsidiary teacher growth programs; and to increase the open and distance learning system so it will reply to the rising demand for education for all ages, across faculty education, professional, and vocational training, course of study, and distance learning.

5.7 Training to Faculty Members

As instructors become ready to implement AR, there are challenges to think about. A number of these problems are general, and instructors won't be addressing them alone. Yet, it's vital for instructors to remember them and present them to directors, technologists, and potential sources of help (Figure 5.7).

5.7.1 Example in Teaching Science: Augmented Reality Map – STEPS

1. Hook
2. Planning and Research

3. Content Creation
4. Productions
5. Evaluations

1. Hook

Students use Aurasma to study cryptograms on a map. The mysterious code triggers recordings and archives made by various students concerning areas on the map. When they see the item, students take a short examination about the video or article. On the off chance that there isn't any student content for these students to review and measure, the educator will create a partner map to share.

2. Planning and Analysis

Utilizing the huge technique, students orchestrate their examination and undertaking. I exploit a clear realistic coordinator and a progression of requests to encourage students to set up an examination. After that, students use books, data sets, and online reference books to look up information on their subject. Depending on your guide's center, subjects could shift from spots to critical brief videos or produce partner degree information that is realistic or a mind map on their theme.

3. Content Creation

Subsequent to doing the investigation, students need to create carefully fabricated products to share through Aurasma. This may be a video, a thinking or mind map, or partner degree information. In the event that students produce a considerations guide or realistic information, you should take of photo or video of their work to move it into Aurasma.

4. Productions

After making their item, students must move their video, picture, or connection onto your Aurasma channel. Students then must create a guide picture that you can utilize (and transfer) based on the trigger picture. I like to advocate making the images a couple of inches in size. I then ask students to frame their images by hand; however, PC produces and composes images as well. Aurasma trigger pictures work best with lots of details.

5. Evaluations

As students complete each progression, and before they "turn in" finished products, I challenge them to complete a quick self-assessment. Regardless of whether students have finished their guide images and associated the images to their

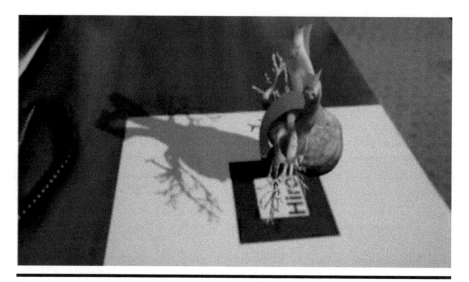

Figure 5.8 Augmented Reality (AR) Demonstration of Beating Heart (https://www.youtube.com/watch?v=9ue1ALMk6aE).

computerized item, the students start investigating and assessing each other's work. This may be casual or part of their formal assessment (Figure 5.8).

5.8 Planning and Administration for Implementation

Requirements for AR within the classroom; nominal AR setup for pretty much any category might include:

- Web Affiliation
- Mobile Devices
- AR Apps
- "Triggers" or "Markers"

5.8.1 Implications of AR

AR connects the virtual world with the real world. It is quality rising apace in each business from social media filters to surgical events. As the word "augment" suggests, AR enhances what we have a tendency to hear, see, and feel. Its classes support numerous technologies. A number of those classes are marker-based AR, markerless AR, projection-based AR, and superimposed AR (Figure 5.9).

There are numerous industries like public safety, tourist services, and recreation that use AR. In the medical field, there are varied AR applications that support the video platform and may project increased hands on a patient. Where a surgery is happening, a senior physician will guide a beginner in his surgery.

Figure 5.9   Augmented Reality for Education.

AR is about to improve the world's standard learning model. It will motivate a change within the location and temporal order of categories and create learning through participation. Today's learning method is far more tuned to interaction and creative thinking. Providing visual representations helps learners to check their data through observations (Figure 5.10).

AR technology has additionally helped students to learn about and perceive their environment. It's providing students with sensible data on subjects like

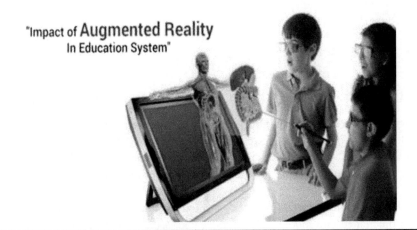

Figure 5.10   Augmented Reality in Education.

mathematics and science. Allow us to inspect a couple of uses of AR within the academic sector.

5.8.2 Practical Data at AR Labs

For numerous reasons, teachers might opt to limit the scope of lab demonstrations. This can be another undeniable fact of the employment of AR technology. With AR, students will perform experiments without needing a physical science laboratory. This can be extraordinarily useful for skilled courses. Students may gather data concerning safety procedures and potential hazards within the science laboratory.

5.9 Augmented Reality Education Apps

AR could be an innovation that overlays smart segments – like content, pictures, video cuts, sounds, and 3D models – onto the real world. Not only will AR improve learning, but it will also give students the freedom to shape their own education. Instructor bookkeepers and innovation coordination experts generally help their kindred teachers to incorporate new advancements into class instruction. Examination of the web tells a scope of online AR applications for almost any subject. A few of those applications support twenty-first century abilities like force, critical thinking, significant reasoning, investigation, composing, and monotonous testing.

- 3DBear
- Catchy Words AR
- CoSpacesEdu
- Froggipedia
- Jig Space
- Moat Boat
- Orb
- World Brush

5.10 Augmented Reality Applications for Education

Google translate has an "AR mode" that allows users to survey unknown dialects. You'll have the option to look up words without a dictionary in various dialects. This application will be convenient for every student and traveler. Star Walk, Sky ORB 3D, and Superb House Journey are applications that allow users to study the skies (Figure 5.11).

They utilize the camera, GPS, and pivoting instrument in smartphones to track down the planets and moons. As you move your screen while illuminating the sky, wonderful bodies will appear with corresponding information like the distance

Figure 5.11 How Augmented Reality Apps Transform User Experience.

from earth, size, and so forth inside expanded reality. In school, we will separate it into three classes of applications: those specific for school kids, those for adolescents, and applications for self-development. We should set out a few examples of AR applications for school kids.

5.10.1 Augmented Reality Applications for School Children

Math Alive, which is established for youths until third grades, requires a PC, camera, and specially written cards. Students, with teacher supervision, put the cards before a camera, activating tally skills (Figure 5.12).

Flashcards of Animal Alphabet is a related AR app, except for learning the alphabet, whereas the use of cards "into life" exhibits live animals with the correct solution. Bugs 3D, ZooKazam (Android & iOS), will teach animal species with animated 3D models and numerous info-graphics.

5.10.2 Platforms to Form AR Content

A class of AR apps are not for academic functions primarily but will function as AR for numerous subjects. Look into a number of the subsequent apps (the list isn't exhaustive).

Figure 5.12   AR Education for Android – APK Download.

■ **Augment** with packages appropriate for academic functions in higher education. Display place offers choices to form 3D models. Furthermore, it has numerous alternative helpful options.

■ ZVR, a robust tool by Z-space comes with an intensive instrument to form academic resources. Students armed with the distinct glasses may act with AR objects, while their strength is utilized by the engineers.

■ Daqri Studio, the app to form AR, comes with samples of teaching applications like Anatomy 4D and parts 4D.

■ Blippar Associate in Nursing is already used for several academic institutions and shared with totally different broadcasting retailers.

■ Aurasma and Layar, engineered by Layar Creator, are the most common and effective instruments to form AR content. They have potential in several areas, not only education.

5.11 Coordinated Utilization of AR Applications

In the past years, improvements in AR and VR innovations have taken some enormous jumps. One such region where AR and VR keep on taking huge steps is e-learning.

1. Consistent Preparation

From the past years, the overall insight towards consistent preparation stays unaltered as the students think of it as a dull, tedious undertaking. With this section of AR and VR in e-learning, expect a turnaround as the students begin cherishing consistent preparation encounters utilizing VR and AR. Here, the students can learn by rehearsing in a vivid virtual climate that can recreate this present reality climate.

For instance, a year ago, we saw the arrival of a VR-based consistent preparation program under the OSHA rules. The preparation happens in a completely delivered and sensible 3D preparing climate –the preparation and evaluation exercises to challenge laborers on their insight into OSHA wellbeing guidelines and consistency (Figure 5.13).

2. Hands-on Preparation

This is an involved technique for preparing students with the ability, information, and skills to execute a reasonable job inside their work environment. While the conventional e-learning procedures come up short in extending to employment opportunity preparation, the utilization of VR and AR is certain to make advances in giving hands-on preparation. Students play as a couple of hands working over a fryer. In addition, students encounter different reenactments that show how to react to situations, how the sales rep and the vendor will react to clashes, and how to oversee large events.

3. Basic Abilities Preparation

VR permits companies to take advantage of VR to prepare specialists for basic abilities. For example, the main airplane producer Boeing utilizes VR innovation to prepare their laborers. Boeing has molded VR pictures of the body of the airplane, with intensive, precise visuals of the wires that must be connected. Learners are

Figure 5.13   Integrated Applications of AR.

(Source: https://playxlpro.com/9-applications-of-ar-and-vr-in-e-learning/)

taken through the unit and see what they need to do. This program brought about a 40% improvement in profitability.

4. Preparing in Unsafe Circumstances

Utility companies like oil and flammable gas, power plants, and substance-producing businesses prepare representatives on their hardware and cycles, as well as for working in dangerous spots like mines, which is risky without acquiring satisfactory abilities and information. The virtual climate created utilizing VR and AR innovation assists the company with preparing students on testing and perilous circumstances. The computer-generated simulation can reproduce the genuine working encounters to prepare the laborers without the dread of committing any errors. Likewise, the student can rehash the learning interaction "n" number of times to acquire dominance over it.

5. Representative Onboarding

Studies have shown that representative onboarding has an immediate connection to work fulfillment and worker maintenance. The representatives are destined to leave the company if there is no established orientation program. Companies are investigating approaches to take advantage of VR and AR in worker onboarding to make the experience more exciting and draw in fresh recruits. Likewise, VR can help recently added team members feel sure about their jobs.

For instance, the well-known web-based learning stage Udemy has a novel onboarding program that utilizes AR innovation to prepare recently added team members and locally train them. The fresh recruits are sent for a scavenger hunt to gather the most extreme number of welcome balloons and outdo the leaderboard. The student learns by moving around, addressing the inquiries, finding out about the organization and its societies, and so on in a fun way. Additionally, students can utilize their cell phones to partake in the onboarding measure.

The future looks extremely fascinating, particularly for the companies in the assembling area, where the fresh recruits can get acquainted with the assembling setup even before they join the company. In the beginning phases of the on-boarding cycle, for example, during the period of pre-enlistment, the companies can permit the fresh recruits to take a virtual visit through the area.

6. Item Preparation

AR and VR can disturb current preparation strategies like study hall or conventional types of e-learning. To prepare laborers on item preparation, the company can incorporate AR and VR innovation and train specialists in a reenacted working climate. This exercise will be more agreeable as laborers are placed in front of the machines, and this prompts improved gathering and upkeep as the student can quickly incorporate the information.

The VR experience incorporates preparing encounters of VR to cover everything from vehicle gathering, preparing for new colleagues, and client care administration. In 2013, a similar organization utilized AR preparation strategies to prepare their laborers to adjust vehicles. The future will see more companies embrace VR and AR to prepare their laborers on fixing machines.

7. Deal Preparation

Outreach groups assume a huge part in the accomplishment of any business. For each company, it is fundamental to guarantee that the outreach group is expertly prepared with deal preparation abilities, item information, and that's just the beginning. With the improvements in AR and VR, this most recent mechanical development makes certain to track down an unmistakable spot in deal preparation.

For instance, there are associations like Virtual Speech that convey VR instructional classes for the outreach group. Here, the sales rep is submerged in a virtual climate where he/she can rehearse his/her selling and exchange abilities with a virtual customer. Various deal situation modules can go into VR, and the sales rep can continue to improve and dominate the expertise.

8. Delicate Abilities Preparation

Delicate abilities are consistently a fundamental component in the professional workplace. In the most recent couple of years, expanding interest for delicate expertise work environments is noticeable as most employees have bosses in the work environment. The conventional preparation innovations of study hall preparation stayed more as a one-size-fits-all methodology of learning as students act differently in similar circumstances.

Utilizing VR and AR for delicate abilities preparation can assist students with taking an individual learning path and making it more relatable. Subsequently, the company can before long see the more extensive utilization of VR and AR in figuring out how to prepare the specialists on delicate subjects. There are now numerous portable applications and assets accessible in the market today that utilize VR and AR innovation to prepare students on different delicate expertise prerequisites like Virtual Orator, Speech Center VR, and Public Speaking Simulator VR.

9. Different Regions

AR and VR, when joined with micro learning technique, is another inventive method to draw in students. We should take a gander at some imaginative methods of utilizing AR and VR exercises for micro learning.

A. Practical Online Assessments:
With VR encounters, the company can plan functional online evaluations as

miniature chunks. The company can decide to incorporate micro learning situations by utilizing VR or AR where the student is needed to execute the things learned and the company can measure the presentation of the student live with real-time input.

B. **VR info graphics:**

VR info graphics are the better approach for making info graphics that convey a vivid encounter to the client.

C. **Virtual Case Considerations:**

The vivid learning experience utilizing AR and VR can assist with creating visual contextual investigations that can remake the situation. The utilization of vivid visuals moves the student to a drawing-in encounter through a content-based contextual analysis.

5.12 Reasons for Using Augmented Reality in Learning

1. Much Better Clarification of Complicated and Abstract Ideas

There is little doubt that your learners can perceive a thought better once they can imagine it. Particularly for tough units, learners can be taught first with 3D representation.

2. Elevated Learner Engagement

AR learning shows a gamified move towards learning; that makes teaching fun. It has an optimistic effect on learners and keeps them engaged.

3. No Further Tools Needed

Today, 95% of teens own Android devices. These could be used for positive results. Adults and teachers don't have to be compelled to buy tools for interactive learning and teaching.

4. Sensible Data

Students will perform well with no physical need for laboratory instruments. This will be primarily useful for skilled courses in life sciences.

5. Accessible Learning

Users of AR applications will study all the time and at any place from their smartphones. They will no longer need paper books, posters, large models, etc.

5.13 Conclusion

AR is employed in many fields. AR in education continues to be new and exciting. AR is an efficient instrument for learning, creating the need for the healthy role of autonomous learning by providing agility and interactivity within the instructional method. We would like to own an interactive teaching-learning method, and this dynamic role of education is predictable with the use of AR in education and the manufacturing of a technologically savvy generation of youths.

Though the probabilities of teaching in AR are wonderful and establish new ways of learning, academics ought to catch the eye of scholars and encourage them to obtain new tools to ascertain their subjects and complicated ideas, and likewise on get sensible skills. Moreover, even older adults can profit from partaking with youngsters in review.

In light of an examination by Digi-Capital investigation and business firm, AR is going to have a billion clients by 2021. Thinking about the expanding nature of AR in training, a nice segment of this client base can involve students, teachers, and various partners inside the instruction exchange.

AR has many benefits in school, and these will be essentially applied in our daily lives. AR's greatest benefit in learning is that it supports interest and propels the student to get a handle on a ton of information. This is regularly the central structure of any learning cycle and makes AR very functional in training.

As seen in this chapter, AR improves abilities, language, and many other things. AR may basically be the long haul of all learning conditions any place information is available. This innovation has made it possible to investigate and get items and subjects in a very strategy that the ordinary instruction frameworks couldn't, and this is regularly why we anticipate it's the more drawn-out term of schooling. Teachers are looking for approaches to help their students learn faster and retain information. AR technology will enable them to do that, providing unbelievable advantages that will prove priceless to students for the remainder of their lives.

References

Antonioli, B. M., Blake, C., & Sparks, K. (2013). Augmented reality applications in education. (2009), 40(2), 96–107, https://doi.org/10.21061/jots.v40i2.a.4.

Azuma, R., Baillot, Y., Behringer, R., & Feiner, S. (2001). Recent advances in augmented reality. *IEEE Computer Graphics and Applications, 21*(6), 34–47.

Azuma, R.T. (1997). A survey of augmented reality. *Teleoperators and Virtual Environments, 6*(4), 355–385.

Braund, M., & Reiss, M. (2006). Towards a more authentic science curriculum: The contribution of out- of -school learning. *International Journal of Science Education, 28*(12), 1373–1388.

Bower, M., Robinson, A., & Grover, D. (1994). Augmented reality in education—Cases, places, and potentials. *Educational Media International*, 1–11.

Cabero-Almenara, J., Fern, M., & Barroso-Osuna, J. (2019). *Heliyon adoption of augmented reality technology by university students Heliyon.* (May). 5(5): e01597. doi: 10.1016/j.heliyon.2019.e01597

Coimbra, M. T., Cardoso, T., & Mateus, A. (2015). Augmented reality: An enhancer for higher education students in math's learning?. *Procedia Computer Science, 67,* 332–339. doi: 10.1016/j.procs.2015.09.277

Cyber Gloves. (2011). Meta motion. http://www.metamotion.com/images/wireless_CG.jpg

Delello, J. A., Mcwhorter, R. R., & Camp, K. M. (2015). Integrating augmented reality in higher education: A multidisciplinary study of student perceptions. *Journal of Educational Multimedia and Hypermedia, 24,* 209–233.

Feiner, S. (2011, 12 2). Augmented reality: A long way off?. Retrieved from Pocket-lint: http://www.pocket-lint.com/news/38869/augmented-reality-interview-steve-feiner

Ghare, A. M., Khan, M. A., Rangwala, M., & Kazi, S. (2017). Augmented reality for educational enhancement. *International Journal of Advanced Research in Computer and Communication Engineering, 6*(3), 232–235. doi: 10.17148/IJARCCE.2017.6352

Hare, O., Barrow, J., Forker, C., Sands, A., Hare, D. O., & Hurst, W. (2019). *Augmented reality for enhancing life science education augmented reality for enhancing life science education.* In: VISUAL 2019 - The Fourth International Conference on Applications and Systems of Visual Paradigms. Italy.

Imamura, M. (2017). *Beyond the limitations of environmental education in Japan.* (11), 3–14. *ISSN: 2320-2653 ISSN: 2320-2653.* (2017). 5(3), 21–28.

Ims, I., Reality, A., Alpha, G., & Alpha, G. (2020). *Prepare online for CAT 2020 Augmented Reality: The future of education.*

Inition. (2011, 12 1). PINCH Gloves. Retrieved from Inition: http://www.inition.co.uk/3D-Technologies/fakespace-labs-pinch-glovesInition. (2011, 12 1). Trivisio M3-Maintenance. Retrieved from Inition: http://inition.co.uk/3D-Technologies/trivisio-m3-maintenance

Kiyokawa, K., Billing Hurst, M., Hayes, S., Gupta, A., Sannohe, Y., & Kato, H. (2002). Communication behaviors of co-located users in collaborative AR interfaces. *IEEE and ACM international symposium on mixed and augmented reality (ISMAR 2002)* (pp. 139–148). Darmstadt, Germany: IEEE Press.

Lee, B. K. (2012). Augmented reality in education and training. 13–22.

Liar Okapis, F., & Anderson, E. F. (2010). *Using augmented reality as a medium to assist teaching in higher education.* (October 2016). doi: 10.2312/eged.20101010

Miller, D. R., & Dousay, T. (2016). *In the classroom.* (May). doi: 10.2458/azu

Nincarean, D., Bilal, M., Dayana, N., Halim, A., & Abdul, H. (2013). Mobile augmented reality: The potential for education. *Procedia - Social and Behavioral Sciences, 103,* 657–664. doi: 10.1016/j.sbspro.2013.10.385

Passig, D. (n.d.). *The future of virtual reality in education: A future oriented meta-analysis of the literature.* 269–293.

Paper, C., & Baldiris, S. (2017). *Augmented reality applications for education: Five directions for future augmented reality applications for education: Five directions for future research.* (June). doi: 10.1007/978-3-319-60922-5

Sirakaya, M., & Sirakaya, D. A. (2018). Trends in educational augmented reality studies: A systematic review. *Journal of Educational Technology, 6*(2), 60–74.

Saltan, F. (2017). The use of augmented reality in formal education: A scoping review. *EURASIA Journal of Mathematics Science and Technology Education, 8223*(2), 503–520. doi: 10.12973/eurasia.2017.00628a

Tanya, (2020). *Augmented reality in education: A way to future ar will become the driver of education systems soon what augmented reality actually is?*. https://www.mobileappdaily.com/2018/08/1/augmented-reality-in-education.

Trondsen, E., Member, B., & Vikings, S. (2019). *Augmented/virtual reality in Nordic/Baltic education, learning and training*. (April), 1–73.

Zhao, Y., & Chen, C. (2016). *The application of augmented reality in university*, Advances in Intelligent Systems Research, 130 6th International Conference on Mechatronics, Computer and Education Informationization (MCEI 2016), 885–888.

Books

https://www.qualcomm.com/media/documents/files/the-mobile-future-of-augmented-reality.pdf presentation slides, Data accessed 1 Oct 2021

Zlatanova, D. I. S. (2002). *Augmented reality technology. GIS technology report 17, Delft, The Netherlands.*

Articles/Chapters in Edited Books

Augmented Reality. Retrieved from Colorado School of Mines Division of Engineering: http://engineering.mines.edu/research/sensing-comm-control/project/?pid=44

Billing Hurst, M. (n.d.). (2002), *Augmented reality in education*. New Horizon for Learning, Seattle.

Bimber, O., Raskar, R., & Inami, M. (2007). Spatial augmented reality. SIGGRAPH 2007 Course 17 Notes. CSM. (2011, 12 2).

Bybee, R.W. et al. (1989) *Science and technology education for the elementary years: Frameworks for curriculum and instruction*. Washington, D.C.: The National Center for Improving Instruction.

Conference Proceedings

In Information & Communication Technology in Science Education 2007/Proceedings of International Scientific Practical Conference, Siauliai.

Internet References

https://dzone.com/articles/augmented-reality-in-education, Date accessed 5 Oct 2021

https://easternpeak.com/blog/augmented-reality-in-education-the-hottest-edtech-trend-and-how-to-apply-it-to-your-business, Date accessed 5 Oct 2021

https://en.wikipedia.org/wiki/Augmented_reality#Possible_applications, Date accessed 5 Oct 2021

https://inc42.com/features/what-is-the-future-of-edtech-and-learning-in-india-from-an-ar-vr-lens/, Date accessed 5 Oct 2021

https://journals.uair.arizona.edu/index.php/itet/article/view/18601/18526, Date accessed 5 Oct 2021

https://naerjournal.ua.es/article/view/v8n2-4#f-491f3a1bf20b, Date accessed 5 Oct 2021

https://www.qualcomm.com/media/documents/files/the-mobile-future-of-augmented-reality.pdf, Date accessed   5 Oct 2021 https://smartglasseshub.com/benefits-of-augmented-reality-in-education/, Date accessed 5 Oct 2021

https://www.analyticsinsight.net/top-10-augmented-and-virtual-reality-trends-to-watch-in-2020/, Date accessed 5 Oct 2021

https://www.augrealitypedia.com/augmented-reality-in-education-increase-student-engagement-classroom, Date accessed 5 Oct 2021

https://www.ebsco.com/blog/article/top-10-augmented-reality-tools-for-the-classroom, Date accessed 5 Oct 2021

https://www.emergingedtech.com/2018/08/multiple-uses-of-augmented-reality-in-education/, Date accessed 5 Oct 2021

https://www.frontiersin.org/articles/10.3389/fpsyg.2018.02086/full, Date accessed 5 Oct 2021

https://www.interaction-design.org/literature/article/augmented-reality-the-past-the-present-and-the-future, Date accessed 5 Oct 2021

https://www.iste.org/explore/In-the-classroom/25-resources-for-bringing-AR-and-VR-to-the-classroom, Date accessed 5 Oct 2021

https://www.profolus.com/topics/advantages-and-disadvantages-of-augmented-reality/, Date accessed 5 Oct 2021

http://www.sony.net/SonyInfo/News/Press/201105/11-058E/ Trivisio. (2011, 12 1)ARvision-3D HMD. Retrieved from Trivisio: http://www.trivisio.com/index.php/products/hmdnte/arvision-3d-hmd, Date accessed 5 Oct 2021

https://www.talk-business.co.uk/2018/07/09/the-benefits-of-augmented-reality-in-education-and-learning-process, Date accessed 5 Oct 2021

https://www.timeshighereducation.com/news/augmented-reality-in-higher-education-five-tips-to-get-started/2018933. article, Date accessed 5 Oct 2021

Chapter 6

Gamification for Education 5.0

D. Ramya Chitra

Assistant Professor, Department of Computer Science, Bharathiar University, Coimbatore, India

Contents

DOI: 10.1201/9781003175896-6

Objectives

This chapter addresses the following objectives:

- Gamification and its importance
- Augmented reality games for education
- Related works in gamification
- Software tools for gamification

Case Studies on Gamification in School Education, Higher Education, Learning Disorder, Corporate learning and the effects on Gamification

---

6.1 Introduction

The introduction of computers and gaming consoles led to the fame of digital games. Video games affected language learning, social science, and physical education compared to science and math (Young et al., 2012). The younger generation spends most of its time playing digital games; hence, it is better to use digital games for learning purposes. Gamification is a technique where gameplay and entertaining elements are added in a non-game environment to raise the involvement of the user with the product or service. This will help users to achieve their targets as well as overcome their negative connection with the system. Gamification uses game-like attributes in the context of education. Action, challenge, and reward are the main constituents for learning through gamification. Action deals with learners carrying out an activity that is related to learning objectives. Learners will be given some challenges that they are supposed to complete within the time limit. By completing the activity successfully, learners will get a reward. Other attributes of gamification include assessment, control, environment, game fiction, human interaction, etc. The control deals with the degree to which the players can alter the game as well as the game alters itself based on the response. For the past four decades, many games for education and gamification systems have been established and used, which were not restricted to age, culture, or subject, and games were very active in enlightening the tasks presented to pupils. The background, context, and skills of the individual vary and have to be identified for effective game-based learning (Kang, Moon, & Diederich, 2019).

Higher efficiency can be achieved in the work environment by redefining the current learning process so that the motivation of the staff can be improved to a great extent. Millennials are behind the changing work environment and will dominate managerial roles throughout the world. Communication and rising social awareness are replacing the way things were done before. To sustain the business world and win it over, communication, collaboration, competency, creativity, and critical thinking are needed, and that can be achieved through gamification technology. This integrates the performance measures, challenges, and rewards that can lead to an energetic workplace (Goethe, 2019). When games have to be applied in the learning domain, many views have to be taken that include perception, conduct, inspiration, affective sociocultural dimensions, etc. This will help developers to design the necessary games based on the learning grounds (Charles, Bustard, & Black, 2011; Plass, Homer, & Charles, 2015).

Educational games should be designed so that learners are able to enhance their knowledge and understanding of intellectual and hands-on skills. Also, the game must consist of evaluation, which should differentiate between game scoring and external and embedded scoring. This will help the learners and designers to come up with the in-game interactions and leads to the success of the game as well as learning. Instructional designers and game developers have to emphasize smart assessment on game-based learning (Ifenthaler, Eseryel, & Ge, 2012). It is used to promote learner behavior changes in non-game designs and improves learner engagement. A planned strategy is needed that emphasizes easing learner commitment through associated game mechanics. The features such as point, badge, progression, etc., are recognized as design components for gamification (Seaborn & Fels, 2015). Gamification is a psychologically driven method, but, from a practical point of assessment, it is a design problem with motivation. When motivation is the target, it is assessed through grades, attendance, etc. The design components have different consequences, such as commitment, involvement, motivation, enjoyment, achievement, accomplishment, performance, and appreciation (Nah, Zeng, Telaprolu,

Ayyappa, & Eschenbrenner, 2014). Design principles such as adapting to various educational purposes, enabling educators to have control over students' commitment, scaling up or down to achieve the needed level of complexity, and maintaining the students' interest by balancing the challenge with skill level are also identified (El-Masri & Tarhini, 2015). Educational games have been designed in applied sciences, basic sciences, social sciences, medical sciences, etc. Educators and innovators who participated in the Education Innovation Conference in 2018 in Bangalore had the opinion that Indian schools must make use of gamification to motivate students towards learning.

Gamification utilizes game features such as searches, tests, stages, and prizes to inspire and involve pupils in the classroom. Given the commitment that pupils sense through gameplay, it is practical to contain features of game strategy to encourage pupils and build a space for complete language tutoring. The policy to be framed for implementing gamification in e-learning has to consider many features, such as ascertaining learners' qualities, defining their objectives, creating educational material and events for multiple enactments, the possibility of playing together with other learners, and adding game features and procedures.

Gamification has several benefits, including cognitive and physical development in adolescents like exercising with an interactive game, accessibility, and increasing level of commitment in classrooms.[1] There will also be increased comfort and retention, tangible progress, resilience to failure, and consistent assignment completion.[2] The gaming applications that are used in simulated and augmented reality environments are also desired in public, service, food, health, and education environments. To achieve this, the tasks that may affect accomplishments in digital environments have to be overcome, and user needs have to be incorporated. Apart from motivation, various disciplines that are related to gaming, learning, and behavioral sciences can also be included (Kocakoyun & Ozdamli, 2018).

There are some negative effects on gamification. For example, the poor interface design of the leaderboard (a high score listing that ranks players according to their success) or point system will make the students bored so that they might leave the platform. Sometimes, gamification prevents students from achieving their targets accidentally so that they lose their confidence. If the target is set too high compared with the abilities of the students, they might get frustrated.

6.2 Augmented Reality Games for Education

AR games can aid novel methods of education and can change learning practice. Integrating game-based learning and gamification into the program will improve the commitment of students and will lead to student-centric learning and improve their learning experiences. For this, the theoretical framework of learning must be clearly understood. Different theories will be suitable for different situations as there is no solitary meaning for learning as it rests on one's perspective. The guidelines for the progress of AR games to be utilized in the learning context – compiling design feedback, creating collaborative shared experiences, utilizing things from real scenarios, and designing the game model – have to be framed (Weerasinghe, Quigley, Ducasse, Pucihar, & Kljun, 2019). To enhance learning capability, the simulated world and real world are fused. Augmented reality can be combined with mobile devices so that the features comprising transferability, where the data transfer from one device to another, are simple. Societal inter-activity, integration that connects different applications and devices to obtain different types of data, context sensitivity for user data protection, and uniqueness can be used (Nincarean, Ali, Halim, & Rahman, 2013).

6.3 Related Works

Erenli (2013) developed a toolkit, QuizeRo, that makes teaching more fun. This tool can be deployed using a QR code scanning device and a GPS device. Experts in the education field can utilize this method to develop scavenger hunts that will meet the requirements of various fields. Educators may be hesitant to use games due to limited resources, game complications, inadaptability for different learning consequences, weak student participation, and difficulty incorporating course structures. Educational games can address these factors when properly designed.

If gamification is properly incorporated into e-learning in higher education there will be a progressive effect such as higher contentment, inspiration, and commitment of the students. In all phases of progress of e-learning, user experience has to be considered. Integrating gamification will result in a higher degree of personalization. Using artificial intelligence (AI) in personalization will result in discovery of the definite activities, errors, and behavioral features of students by professors so that e-learning can be adjusted through gamification (Urh, Vukovic, Jereb, & Pintar, 2015). AI can support professors to find out if there is any dis-traction to students from their continuous learning and will lead to improved user engagement and sustained learning. The chances of gamification and dynamic difficulty adjustment grounded on multimodal learning analytics in homework is discussed. Personalized assignments are used to analyze the above technology on the student's inspiration and engagement. An educational facility to provide custom-made learning pathways for data science is proposed for individuals who want to be proficient in data science. The context of the practitioner is analyzed and matched with the education components, and gamification is used to reinforce practitioner engagement. Game elements such as skill trees, non-linear learning paths, storylines, rewards, and characters are used. An EDISON framework is applied to identify 19 professions, whereas the contribution from all participants was used to identify learning units and their relation to the professions (Hee, Zicari, Tolle, & Manieri, 2016).

Clear learning purposes, an apt choice of vital terms, and conversion of events into mission challenges have to be used to design a gamified vocabulary curriculum that will result in higher order thinking skills as well as encourage students and create a space for vocabulary education. Contributions to improving instructional design using gamification are presented. Some recommendations, such as focusing on students, picking one or two game mechanics, scalability, play, and having fun, are given (Hung, 2017). Kingsley and Grabner-Hagen (2017) have given snap-shots, illustrations, and recommendations for daily training of vocabulary and bringing students into line with the levels of Bloom's nomenclature. Also, the provision of gamification for learner sovereignty and mastery is discussed.

Boyinbode (2018) embraced the use of a gamification-based English language learning technique for motivating learners to learn vocabulary. In this system, the vocabulary recommendation module will suggest the vocabulary centered on the stage of the game the player is playing; the test and assessment modules test and evaluate the performance of the learner based on the dictionary in the database. Low completion and high dropout of students for Massive Open Online Courses (MOOC) led to flipped MOOC, where a flipped classroom approach based on gamification and analytics was applied. Through this, the authors declared that the MOOC can be changed from a content-oriented delivery mechanism to a custom-made communication and engagement learning environment (Klemke, Eradze, & Antonaci, 2018). The pervasive presence of technology has moved from traditional classroom teaching to the digital teaching environment, by which it incorporates the game features that resulted in user attention, motivation towards the goals, promoting competition, effective teamwork, and communication. The higher education institution employing this methodology will improve students' commitment, motivation, and performance (Subhash & Cudney, 2018).

iMoodle, a smart Moodle based on games that use education-based analytics, was developed to afford a control panel for teachers to regulate the education process and increase students' success rate as well as find at-risk students by notification (Denden et al., 2019). Antonaci, Klemke, and Specht (2019) gathered the game features and their effects into six areas – presentation, encouragement, commitment, approach towards gamification, teamwork, and social consciousness. Effects of badges varied according to gender and personality and were viewed as restrictive. Badges may negatively affect motivation and engagement. Effects of leaderboards differed based on whether they triggered communal comparison and race among students. Effects of points, score, and ranking improved users' engagement to take on challenging tasks. To increase skills and retention with employee satisfaction, gamification using machine learning and statistical models can be used. Based on this, an improved gamified model was designed that made use of the original data, Weibull statistical distribution, K-means clustering algorithm, and machine learning with reward systems. Psychological theories played a significant role to harness user engagement; hence, they were used in the gaming application (Shanmugalingam, 2019).

The effectiveness of gamification compared to traditional learning for health profession education concerning the outcomes of the patients, familiarity, expertise, professional assertiveness, and fulfillment as well as financial effects of education were evaluated. MEDLINE, EMBASE, Web of Knowledge, Allied Health Literature, and more databases were searched, and the data were extracted in two different studies. A study showed some comparisons between gaming and digital education of healthcare professionals to regulate blood pressure in a group of patients. Through many studies, it was found that serious gaming may advance skills, knowledge, and satisfaction (Gentry et al., 2019). Gamification can enhance the education process by assisting both teachers and learners to attain objectives like students' motivation, analysis of students' knowledge, students' attitude, etc. Theoretical approaches for this methodology are described, and a conceptual model is given to improve the quality of teaching, especially in management (Silva, Rodrigues, & Leal, 2019).

6.4 General Software Tools for Gamification

Many tools are available for gamification. The popular ones are listed below.[3]

i. KnowRe

This math program for school students delivers a step-by-step learning map and game-like feature that adds pleasant to dull mathematical calculations.

ii. Beeup

This is an online stage through which students can answer corporate case studies that are based on real-world complications of Beeup's company. This program is open to everyone, and students receive a certificate after solving ten case studies.

iii. Socrative

This is a game-based classroom platform that is diverse and can be adapted to all platforms. It has three different ways – the query-based game type, space race that combines accuracy and speed, and exit ticket that is used at the end of the chapter for assessment.

iv. Duolingo

This is a free online mobile language learning service, and the education is gamified for users to enjoy learning.[4]

v. MineCraft Edu

This tool is designed for classroom learning, which offers a cloud-based solution for hosting the server, and a library of lessons and activities are hosted together so that students and teachers can join and play together.

6.5 Case Studies and Tools for Gamification

Case studies and tools for gamification in education are available in the literature, and a few are listed here. This section classifies the case studies into school education, higher education, learning disorder, and corporate learning. Finally, case studies on the effect of gamification in education are also given.

6.5.1 Gamification in School Education

In school education, gamification for music, biology, mathematics, financial literacy, and vocabulary learning are given.

6.5.1.1 Music

A case study on gamification in teaching music was conducted in some schools located at Padro da Legua, Matosinhos, and the quality of learning was measured for eight weeks. In this study, multimedia materials were used for instrumental practice and backing vocals. The students can access the resources in two ways: (i) a task that is presented will be monitored by the teacher in the classroom setting, and (ii) students can have access to the multimedia resources through the Moodle platform. Another method was used where the students were taught without the multimedia or gaming techniques. Inspiration was improved in the group when students used the multimedia materials; the group that used games developed parallel skills in adjacent areas such as communication and concealed curriculum (Gomes, Figueiredo, & Bidarra, 2014).

6.5.1.2 Biology

A study presented a technique, "Which Plant Am I", that will increase plant knowledge and help students to become more familiar with plants. The game was verified with two categories of students, and the category of students in the classroom were motivated through the active and playful learning process (Borsos, 2018).

6.5.1.3 Mathematics

A badge scheme for middle school students comprising 36 seventh class students and 15 eighth class students was analyzed for learning applied mathematics from an intelligent tutoring system. The measures, such as mastery, performance approach, and avoidance goals, were evaluated, and both optimistic and undesirable effects of using the badges were analyzed. It was found that it influenced the learning both positively and negatively, and it was different across varying learner performance ranges (Abramovich, Schunn, & Higashi, 2013).

Leometry application teaches fundamental geometric shapes to the wards of elementary school. A story is used to get the players involved in an adventure in the African Savannah. The player is aided by a dung beetle, who offers tasks in geometry and delivers responses and suggestions. Two levels are used, where level 0 is the visualization level where students can learn elementary shapes. At level 1, students can analyze the shape based on its characteristics. The story of the game, tasks of the pedagogy, and animal deceptions are disseminated around a geographical area. The students find it interesting and enjoyable while learning geometric shapes. The dung beetle will present various geometric challenges and gives feedback as well as hints. Several screens are available for students. One screen has text, image, and sound. There are two screens where the student has to identify a valid geometric shape. The fourth screen will show the points earned by the student, and the fifth and sixth screens are used to advance in the story (Laine, 2018).

Mathland application uses entertainment and novelty. It was created for students by a special education teacher in Michigan, United States. The math course is broken down into 20 levels and has a final mastery test to find out whether the student has completed the level. In the first two years, attendance increased by 13%, and in the first three years, performance increased by 22%.

KnowRe, a math adaptive learning program for middle and high school students, offers a phased learning map and game-like features so that it adds excitement over dull mathematical equations. It finds the weak areas of students, and the teacher can keep track of the accomplishments of students.

6.5.1.4 Financial Literacy

A financial literacy program, PlayMoolah, was developed for pupils aged six and above. The game uses avatars, incentives, leveling, and challenges and covers the features of financial literacy, such as earning, spending, saving, and investing, and also includes life skills, such as goal setting and collaboration, with the involvement of parents and their guidance. It was found that through this program, there was a 78% increase in young people who wanted to increase their savings (Huang & Soman, 2013).

6.5.1.5 Vocabulary Learning

A case study was led in Macau to figure out the outcome of using gamification while learning vocabulary, and it was found that five to sixteen exposures were needed to learn vocabulary in a second language. The investigators believed that the use of games in vocabulary learning helped because they involved repeated failures. Web 2.0 games, namely "Fling the Teacher" and "Jeopardy", which facilitated vocabulary retention, were used to learn vocabulary for the students at a tertiary institution in Macau. Feedback was collected from 91 freshmen. Students preferred technology to learn as it was fun and exciting and facilitated vocabulary retention and hence enhanced learning.[5]

6.5.2 Gamification in Higher Education

In higher education, case studies on information studies, computer science, computer organization and cloud computing, library, Unified Modeling Language (UML), computer games, introduction to a computer course, the entire curriculum of vocational schools, factory management, manufacturing training, software development, French language, software engineering, Web development, and an electrical engineering course are given.

6.5.2.1 Information Studies

Professor Clifford Lampe at the University of Michigan used gamification principles for Introduction to Information Studies comprising 200 students. Choice, rapid feedback, collaborative processes, and competition were found to be effective for gamification. To engage in the video games, the users had to choose their path, i.e., the students were given the option to play out their assignments, and this was integrated into the class. Students created a quest log at the beginning of the semester so that they could select future quests. Also, higher level assignments were integrated and were available only when the lower level assignments were completed. It was found that the students were able to hold the facts for an extensive period.[6]

6.5.2.2 Computer Science

A didactic experiment of executing numerous gamification methods into the didactic procedure for a computer science course at a technical university was performed for one semester. The outcomes of the experiment were discussed on 62 students of the first year of the post-graduate program who were separated into four diverse clusters. Two clusters were gamified using modest procedures such as points, leaderboards, and badges, while the remaining tracked the traditional academic rating system. At the end of the semester, the outcomes of the groups comprising attendance, number of added chores accomplished, the grade average, etc., were collected and analyzed. The authors found that gamification can improve student commitment and quality of education when the gamification elements, such as points, leaderboards, and badges, were used (Laskowski & Badurowicz, 2014).

6.5.2.3 Computer Organization and Cloud Computing

Computer organization, an undergraduate course, and cloud computing, a post-graduate course, was gamified in the Delft University of Technology. A point system, badges, status, social game patterns, and cracking added assignments were used to increase the commitment of students throughout the period. Gamification was associated with a rise in the pass percentage of students, and more than 75% of 450 students passed in the first attempt (Josup & Epema, 2014).

6.5.2.4 Library

Lemontree is a library game that focuses on libraries in educational institutions, and a trial was led at the University of Huddersfield. It was observed that students made use of the library materials effectively, and the game facilitated friendly competition among the students and the departments (Armstrong, 2013). These types of applications will increase commitment with the publisher's directory, motivate society associates to discover the worth of their membership deals, and motivate pupils to attach with on-campus education sources.

6.5.2.5 Unified Modeling Language (UML)

The gamified course metamodel was used in a UML paper, and gamified features, such as points, coins, things, badges, leaderboards, content locking, and dealing, were specified for undergraduate computer science students of the Kaunas University of Technology. It was found that the grades of the students were increased, and there was an improvement in the students' motivation by applying gamification (Jurgelaitis, Ceponiene, Ceponis, & Drungilas, 2018).

6.5.2.6 Computer Games

A course on computer games as part of Cross Media bachelor's degree curriculum was planned like a game. Thirty-five students were registered for the course, and 66% of the students passed with a positive result. The game features, such as goals, avatars, XPs, scoreboards, levels, luck, collaboration, competition, and feedback, and the game vocabulary, such as players, game master, mission, big boss fight, and levels, were used instead of pedagogical terms for the survey that comprised 12 face-to-face meetings and online learning homework. Students agreed that the course of game design must be based on teamwork and not on competition (Sillaots, 2015).

6.5.2.7 Mathematics

The outcomes of gamification on learner accomplishment and their approaches when incorporated into the curriculum were found via a study that used a quantitative research methodology and experimental design using pretest-posttest experimental as well as control groups. Ninety-seven members from the

Department of Elementary Mathematics Education of the University in Turkey in 2014–2015 were involved in this study and proved that this technique had a good influence on the accomplishments and approaches of the learners towards lessons (Yildirim, 2017).

6.5.2.8 Introduction to Computing Course

A case study was performed on students of STEM taking an Introduction to Computing Course with attention on gaming activities comprising short as well as long courses. Five hundred one students registered for four semesters, and 15 courses were involved in the study. Qualitative content analysis was used to categorize the course appraisal and third-party remarks into emerging themes and patterns, and the lecture subjects found were knowledgeable, demonstrative, behavioral, physical, and societal engagements. The participation was stimulated by course-long subjects such as attendance, administration of anxiety, task accomplishment, timely response, mastery of the material, and course accomplishment. The gamification system resulted in an increased number of registrations as well as mandated curriculum courses. The case study also addressed the students' willingness to use their devices. It was found that focus on lecture engagement provided an immersive feedback environment that motivated students (Machajewski, 2017).

6.5.2.9 Vocational Schools

A study was conducted for students of higher vocational schools in China. To enhance the effectiveness of teaching and to improve students' commitment, Layout and Management of Distribution Center was developed, which integrates gamifying into teaching for the whole curriculum. Small games were planned for each class so that students could learn information about the games. It was found that systemization, gamification, and immersion had to be concentrated on while designing teaching methodology. Also, case studies should be designed so that they comply with the interests of the students. The game-driven model of the curriculum was used in Shijiazhuang Posts and Telecommunications Technical College, and the students contributed to all the events positively, and the assessment indexes were also enhanced. Through the model, it was found that outstanding effects were achieved and feasible in higher education also (Wang, Wang, & Hu, 2017).

6.5.2.10 Factory Management

A case study was conducted with Lego Mindstorms in factory management teaching, which led to greater involvement in university courses and inspired the progress of societal, personal, and practical skills of the students when the game concept was used for handling manufacturing. The method utilized a level-based storyline with guidelines and objectives using the physical objects of Lego Mindstorms. The sectional features of Lego supported imagination by having diverse groupings so that students worked in an extremely problem-focused approach. These features increased inspiration and deepened students' understanding of production engineering (Muller, Reise, & Seliger, 2015).

6.5.2.11 Manufacturing Training

A gamification training platform was used for students undertaking manufacturing shopfloor training at Nanyang Polytechnic, Singapore, where a simulated industrial shopfloor similar to the real shopfloor situated in the school was designed. In this training, students used several game scenarios and exercise tasks, such as workshop safety, CNC machine introduction, and dynamics. To complete the tasks, students had to find the right machines as well as operations for a given job, including turning, drilling, grinding, etc., through which the students were able to understand the functions in depth. A pilot study was conducted in the second semester involving 134 students from four classes of engineering diploma students, where their understanding level was measured and their advancement was checked using the evaluation feature with immediate feedback. Through the technical quizzes and game feedback survey, the outcomes showed that gamification provided a harmless environment for students without creating any errors. It was also efficient in helping the weak learners compared to classroom teaching, which was found to be less effective (Zhiqiang et al., 2019).

6.5.2.12 Software Development

Software development education forms an image of difficult programming; gamification can ease it. GipHouse, a software development company, has been used to present and analyze gamification for a case study, which increased the programming activity of students learning it. A lesser technique of gamifying the system rewards users for activities with points, and through this motivator, pupils will learn what is needed and be encouraged to achieve it. The game characteristics, such as points and leaderboards, have been used with the tool RedMine, and it was found that there was a positive change in the actions they performed on RedMine (Buisman & van Eekelen, 2014).

6.5.2.13 French Language

Explorez developed for first-year university French students connects the break between gaming and education through query-based education and augmented reality. This application changes the university into a simulated francophone world where students intermingle with characters, objects, and media simultaneously as they enhance their expertise in the French language. Most of the students gave feedback on the tool as amusing, valuable, inspiring, and applicable. The study was conducted on a small test group and demonstrated that game-based learning can be positive motivation for pupils (Perry, 2015).

6.5.2.14 Software Engineering

A gamification framework was designed for a software engineering group of students. A case study was led where the qualitative data were examined using grounded theory procedure. It was found that there was enhanced content understanding, preservation, and summing up. There was positive alteration in the study dynamics and less time needed for studying. Thirty volunteer students from three software engineering classes of the 2015 first semester were involved in the study. Scores and attendance rates were improved when related to the non-contributing students. The comments of the students on the game elements were related to quizzes, quests, and the point system. The students stated that the application was valuable for assisting their education process.[7]

6.5.2.15 Web Development and Electrical Engineering Course

A study was conducted on students learning a Web development course at the Brno University of Technology and an electrical engineering course at KU Leuven. BombsQuery was the assignment developed and given to students to handle an introduction to jQuery. The students had to remove bombs in the field by writing jQuery code. CLR, the current surf project, combined 3D visualization and game elements. Students could interact with the visualization tool and find out the influence of altering the circuit components. Both the applications increased student engagement (Pastushenko, 2019).

6.5.2.16 Technology Course

A case study was led for Cogent, a virtual economy system that covered four years for students undergoing a B.S (technology) course. The study cited the positive effects of gamification in education, such as increased commitment and engagement, and it was found that when the game was taken away, motivation was lowered. Meaningful gamification was applied that makes networks between the in-game elements and non-game elements so that users can maintain their intrinsic motivation. Focus groups and personal interviews were directed at the end of the study, and it was found that the program got positive results for motivation and commitment (Chen, Burton, Vorvoreanu, & Whittinghill, 2015).

A gamified application was implemented for Dutch University students of 101 courses to learn important facts about their program. Feature feedback and session limit was used for this application, and student engagement was found to increase with generic feedback compared to personalized feedback, whereas meeting boundaries was used to stop users from overdoing the game. It is suggested that the careful design of game procedures, such as feedback and session limit, can encourage play through game methods and also increase students' commitment towards learning (Welbers et al., 2019).

6.5.3 Gamification for Students with Learning Disorders

A case study was conducted for 12 weeks that involved seven dyslexic students and two teachers for the program class Dojo that uses avatars and badges to find out the effect of gamification. The students, parents, and teachers were interviewed after some time, and it was found that the motivation level was increased when using the educational software compared to traditional teaching (Googch, Vasalou, Benton, & Khaled, 2016).

6.5.4 Gamification in Corporate Training

A gamified path was created that provides an interesting learning journey where the features of the code of behavior are denoted with diverse sites of industry. The trainee completes learning one place, which comprises a quiz to get points and a passport stamp so that the trainee can go to another location. The trainee has to go through all six locations to complete the game. This imaginative instructional design approach instills an increased level of commitment for the course.[8]

To motivate higher commitment towards anti-corruption employee training, gamification was used, and a field trial was conducted with 158 employees of a multinational bank. It was found that the employees preferred gamified training, which increased their knowledge of the bank's anti-corruption policies, and the less experienced employees with this type of training outperformed the employees with more experience (Baxter, Holderness, & Wood, 2016).

Deloitte Leadership Academy is an online training program for Deloitte employees and clients. Badges and leaderboards were introduced for participation and top achievers. Due to the integration of gamification, there was a 37% increase in weekly usage statistics and a 46% growth in the number of users attending the academy daily.[9]

6.5.5 Effect of Gamification

Gamification related to inspiration and accomplishment in a community college microbiology class was investigated. Questionnaires that included the Instructional Materials Motivation Survey and Flow Experience studied students' level of inspiration. The effect of demographic features comprising culture, gender, and age on students' accomplishment was also studied. Sixty-two candidates of the 2012 semesters over 18 years of age were involved in this study. Students showed enhancement in inspiration levels and test scores after participating in the educational game (Rouse, 2013).

A case study was conducted to find learning inspiration, intellectual load, and learning concern using the Gamification Software Engineering Education Learning System (GSEELS). Structural Equation Modeling covers a survey on the scales of gamification learning, cognitive load, learning anxiety, and academic performance. The recommendations of the study while using the gamified approach were (i) students' satisfaction increased, (ii) students productively reviewed the material they learned, (iii) students' cognitive load was reduced, and (iv) parents were encouraged to allow their children to play games (Su, 2016).

Gaming features were incorporated into education, and the contribution towards societal problems and gender equality in education was analyzed based on the representations and discourse of the trainee teachers comprising 41 members. Semi-structured interviews and focus groups were used to collect the data. The focus questions were based on the idea and procedural applications of gamification; setting of implementations; educational potential; and curriculum, gender inequalities, and gamification. Mixed-method research based on transcription, coding, classification, and examination of the data obtained from interviews, the study of two clusters, and the outcomes achieved showed that gamification can be used in the initial, development, and final phases of education, and gender analysis is required for social science teaching. Thus, using gamification reduced some social problems like gender inequality and also encouraged teachers to design the curriculum towards teaching the social problems mentioned above (Sánchez & Trigueros 2019).

6.6 Conclusion

Gamification makes students develop a positive attitude towards learning and also enhances their motivation and commitment towards learning. The biggest challenge for education is to sustain students' motivation by considering aspects such as game elements, learning activities, goals, and reliability of outcomes. There are many game features like points, badges, avatars, and leaderboards that can be integrated into the application, but all of these do not have to be integrated at all the times. Depending upon the application and the circumstances, the needed game elements can be integrated into the application.

There are some challenges while designing the game for learning purposes because playing games is time-consuming. When integrated into education, the time consumption will be expensive as much of the time is not available in schools or colleges. Students may also focus more on winning than on learning opportunities that are provided by gamification.[10] Language and cultural barriers have to be broken down using translation solutions. There are educational games that are money oriented, and these games have to be properly chosen. These factors have to be taken into account while planning or choosing the game.

Thus, to achieve learning objectives, increase the motivation of learners, and engage students in a friendly, competitive environment, gamification needs to be implemented in education. It also provides a positive change in behavior and attitude towards learning. Students learn the subjects enjoyably and productively. As social elements are added in the applications, teamwork is promoted in the classroom, and students are motivated to exchange their ideas and experiences with their fellow classmates. Teachers also can easily assess the performance of students from different levels and accordingly plan the lesson.

Notes

1. Ashley Deese, 5 Benefits of Gamification, https://ssec.si.edu/stemvisions-blog/5-benefits-gamification [accessed on 26 April 2020]
2. Marcus Guido, 5 Easy Steps for Gamification in Education, https://www.prodigygame.com /blog/gamification-in-education/, [accessed on 26 April 2020]
3. Gabriela Kiryakova, Nadezhda Angelova, Lina Yordanova, Gamification in Education, https://www.sun.ac.za/english/learning-teaching/ctl/Documents/Gamification%20in %20education.pdf, [accessed on 26 April 2020]
4. Priyanka Gupta, 2016. Tools, Tips, and Resources Teachers Must Know to Learn About Gamification of Education, https://edtechreview.in/trends-insights/insights/22 93-gamification-of-education [accessed on 26 April 2020]
5. Sze Lui, LAM, Use of gamification in vocabulary learning: A case study in Macau, CELC Symposium, University of Macau. http://www.nus.edu.sg/celc/research/books/4 th%20Symposium%20proceedings/13).%20Sze%20Lui.pdf
6. Andrew Stott and Carman Neustaedter, http://clab.iat.sfu.ca/pubs/Stott-Gamification.pdf [accessed on 29 April 2020]
7. Patricia Gomes Fernandes Matsubara, Caroline Lima Correa da Silva, Game elements in a software engineering study group: a case study, http://www.facom.ufms.br/ ~patricia/publicacoes/2017/camera-ready-icse.pdf [accessed on 29 April 2020]
8. Asha Pandey, 2018. Case Study – Creating Highly Engaging Corporate Compliance Training with Gamification, https://www.eidesign.net/case-study-creating-highly-engaging-corporate-compliance-training-gamification/ [accessed on 5 May 2020].
9. Gamification and the Future of Education, https://www.worldgovernmentsummit.org/ api/publications/document?id=2b0d6ac4-e97c-6578-b2f8-ff0000a7ddb6 [accessed on 26 April 2020].
10. Adrian Hallberg, 2017. Gamification In Education (The Good And The Bad), https://www.inwhatlanguage.com/gamification-in-education/

References

Abramovich, S., Schunn, C., & Higashi, R. M. (2013). Are Badges Useful in Education?: It Depends upon the Type of Badge and Expertise of Learner. Educational technology, research, and development, *61*(2), 217–232. Springer, New York, http://128.192.17.1 91/EMAT7050/articles/AbromovichEtAl.pdf

Antonaci, A., Klemke, R., & Specht, M. (2019). The effects of gamification in online learning environments: A systematic literature review. *Informatics*, *6*(32), 1–22. doi: 10.3390/informatics6030032

Armstrong, D. (2013). The new engagement game: The role of gamification in scholarly publishing. Springer *Learned Publishing, 26*(4), 253–256. doi: 10.1087/20130403

Baxter, R. J., Holderness, D. K., & Wood, D. A. (2016). The effects of gamification on corporate compliance training: A field experiment of true office anti-corruption training programs. Available at SSRN: https://ssrn.com/abstract=2766683 or 10.2139/ssrn.2766683

Borsos, E. (2018). The gamification of elementary school biology: A case study on increasing understanding of plants. *Journal of Biological Education, 53*(5), 492–505. doi: 10.1080/00219266.2018.1501407

Boyinbode, O. (2018). Development of a gamification based English vocabulary mobile learning system. *International Journal of Computer Science and Mobile Computing, 7*(8), 183–191.

Buisman, A. L. D., & van Eekelen, M. C. J. D. (2014). Gamification in educational software development. *CSERC'14*. Berlin, Germany. doi: 10.1145/2691352.2691353

Charles, M. T., Bustard, D., & Black, M. (2011). Experiences of promoting student engagement through game-oriented learning framework. In M. Ma., A. Oikonomou, & L. C. Jain (Eds.), *Serious games and edutainment applications* (pp. 425–446). Springer. London. doi: 10.1007/978-1-4471-2161-9

Chen, Y., Burton, T., Vorvoreanu, M., & Whittinghill, D. (2015). Cogent: A case study of meaningful gamification in education with virtual currency. *International Journal of Emerging Technologies in Learning (IJET), 10*(1), 39–45. doi: 10.3991/ijet.v10i1.4247

Denden, M., Tlili, A., Essalmi, Fathi, Jemni, M., Chang, M., & RonghuaiHuang, K. (2019) iMoodle: An intelligent gamified moodle to predict "at-risk" students using learning analytics approaches. In A. Tlili, & M. Chang (Eds.), *Data analytics approaches in educational games and gamification systems*. Singapore: Springer.

Dichev, C., & Dicheva, D. (2017). Gamifying education: What is known, what is believed, and what remains uncertain: A critical review. *International Journal of Educational Technology in Higher Education, 14*(9). doi: 10.1186/s41239-017-0042-5

El-Masri, M., & Tarhini, A. (2015). A Design Science Approach To Gamify Education: From games to platforms. ECIS 2015 Research-in-Progress Papers. Paper 48.

Erenli, K. (2013). Gamify your teaching – Using location-based games for educational purposes. *International Journal of Advanced Corporate Learning, 6*(2), 22–27. doi: 10.3991/ijac.v6i2.2960

Gentry, S. V., Gauthier, A., Ehrstrom, B. E., Wortley, D., Lilienthal, A., Car, L. T., Dauwels-Okutsu, S., Nikolaou, C. K., Zary, N., Campbell, J., & Car, J. (2019). Serious gaming and gamification education in health professions: Systematic review. *Journal of Medical Internet Research, 21*(3). doi: 10.2196/12994

Gomes, C., Figueiredo, M., & Bidarra, J. (2014). Gamification in teaching music: Case study. EduRe'14, Universidade Politecnica de Valencia, Espanha.

Googch, D., Vasalou, A., Benton, L., & Khaled, R. (2016). Using gamification to motivate students with Dyslexia. *CHI 2016*. doi: 10.1145/2858036.2858231

Hee, K., Zicari, R. V., Tolle, K., & Manieri, A. (2016). *Tailored data science education using gamification*. 8th International Conference on Cloud Computing Technology and Science, 1, 12–15 Dec 2016, Luxembourg, pp. 627–632. doi: 10.1109/CloudCom.2016.0108

Huang, W., & Soman, D. (2013). A Practitioner's Guide to Gamification of education. Rotman School of Management, University of Toronto. Retrieved from https://inside.rotman.utoronto.ca/behaviouraleconomicsinaction/files/2013/09/GuideGamificationEducationDec2013.pdf

Hung, A. C. Y. (2017). A critique and defense of gamification. *Journal of Interactive Online Learning, 15*(1), 57–72.

Ifenthaler, D., Eseryel, D., & Ge, X. (2012). Assessment for game-based learning. In D. Ifenthaler, D. Eseryel, & X. Ge (Eds.), *Assessment in game-based learning* (pp. 1–8). New York, NY: Springer. doi: 10.1007/978-1-4614-3546-4_1

Josup, A., & Epema, D. H. J. (2014). *An experience report on using gamification in technical higher education.* Proceedings of the 45th ACM technical symposium on Computer Science education. doi: 10.1145/2538862.2538899

Jurgelaitis, M., Ceponiene, L., Ceponis, J., & Drungilas, V. (2018). Implementing gamification in a university level UML modeling course: A case study. *Computer Applications in Engineering Education, 27*(2), 332–343. doi: 10.1002/cae.22077

Kang, J., Moon, J., & Diederich, M. (2019). Educational games and gamification: From foundations to applications of data analytics. In:A. Tlili M. Chang (Eds.), Data analytics approaches in educational games and gamification systems (pp. 3–26). Springer. Singapore

Kingsley, T. L., & Grabner-Hagen, M. M. (2017). Vocabulary by gamification. *The Reading Teacher, 71*(5), 545–555. doi: 10.1002/trtr.1645

Klemke, R., Eradze, M., & Antonaci, A. (2018). The flipped MOOC: Using gamification and learning analytics in MOOC design—A conceptual approach. *Education Sciences, 8*(25), 1–13. doi: 10.3390/educsci8010025

Kocakoyun, S., & Ozdamli, F. (2018). A review of research on gamification approach in education. In R. Morese, S. Palermo, & J. Nervo (Eds.) *Socialization – A multidimensional perspective.* doi: 10.5772/intechopen.74131 IntechOpen. London.

Laine, T. H. (2018). Mobile educational augmented reality games: A systematic literature review and two case studies. *Computers, 7*(1). 19. MDPI. Switzerland. doi: 10.3390/computers7010019

Laskowski, M., & Badurowicz, M. (2014). Gamification in higher education: A case study, human capital without borders: Knowledge and learning for quality of life. Proceedings of the Management, Knowledge and Learning International Conference 2014. ToKnowPress.

Machajewski, S. T. (2017). Application of gamification in a college STEM introductory course: A case study (Ph.D. Thesis, Thesis North Central University).

Muller, B. C., Reise, C., & Seliger, G. (2015). Gamification in factory management education—A case study with Lego Mindstorms. *Procedia CIRP, 26*, 121–126. doi: 10.1016/j.procir.2014.07.056

Nah, F. F.-H., Zeng, Q., Telaprolu, V. R., Ayyappa Padmanabhuni, A., & Eschenbrenner, B. (2014). Gamification of education: A review of literature. *Lecture Notes in Computer Science, 8527*, 401– 409.

Nincarean, D., Ali, M. B., Halim, N. D. A., & Rahman, M. H. A. (2013). *Mobile augmented reality: The potential for education.* 13th International Educational Technology Conference, *103*, pp. 657–664.

Pastushenko, O. (2019). Gamification in assignments: Using dynamic difficulty adjustment and learning analytics to enhance education. *CHI'19 Doctoral Consortium*, October 22–25, 2019, Barcelona, Spain.

Perry, B. (2015). Gamifying French Language Learning: A case study examining a quest-based, augmented reality mobile learning tool. *Procedia-Social and Behavioral Sciences, 174*, 2308–2315.

Plass, J. L., Homer, B. D., & Kinzer, C. K. (2015). Foundations of game-based learning. *Educational Psychologist, 50*(4), 258–283.

Rouse, K. E. (2013). Gamification in science education: The relationship of educational games to motivation and achievement (Ph.D. dissertation, The University of Southern Mississippi).

Sanchez, D. O., & Trigueros, I. M. G. (2019). Gamification, social problems and gender in the teaching of social sciences: Representations and discourse of trainee teachers. *Plos One.* doi: 10.1371/journal.pone.0218869

Seaborn, K. & Fels, D. I. (2015). Gamification in theory and action: A survey. *International Journal of Human-Computer Studies, 74*, 14–31. doi: 10.1016/j.ijhcs.2014.09.006

Shanmugalingam, J. (2019). Gamification and predictive analytics for the next generation of workers (M.Sc. thesis, University of Alberta). doi: 10.7939/r3-kqxa-ay52

Sillaots, M. (2015). *Gamification of higher education by the example of computer games course.* The Seventh International Conference on Mobile, Hybrid and Online Learning. pp. 62–68.

Silva, R. J. R., Rodrigues, R. G., & Leal, C. T. P. (2019). Gamification in management education: A systematic literature review. *BAR – Brazilian Administration Review, 16*(2). doi: 10.1590/1807-7692bar2019180103

Su, C.-H. (2016, August). The effects of students' motivation, cognitive load and learning anxiety in gamification software engineering education: A structural equation modeling study. *Multimedia Tools and Applications, 75*(16), 10013–10036. doi:10.1007/s11042-015-2799-7

Subhash, S., & Cudney, E. A. (2018). Gamified learning in higher education: A systematic review of the literature. *Computers in Human Behavior, 78*, 192–206. doi: 10.1016/j.chb.2018.05.028

Urh, M., Vukovic, G., Jereb, E., & Pintar, R. (2015). *The model for introduction of gamification into e-learning in higher education.* 7th World Conference on Educational Sciences Novotel Athens Convention Center, Athens, Greece. In: Procedia – Social and Behavioral Sciences, *197*, pp. 388–397.

Wang, F., Wang, Y., & Hu, X. (2017). Gamification teaching reform for higher vocational education in China: A case study on layout and management of distribution center. *International Journal of Emerging Technologies in Learning, 12*(09), 130–144. doi: 10.3991/ijet.v12.i09.7493

Weerasinghe, M., Quigley, A., Ducasse, J., Pucihar, K. C., & Kljun, M. (2019). Educational augmented reality games. In V. Geroimenko (Ed.), *Augmented reality games II: The gamification of education, medicine, and art* (pp. 3–32). Springer Nature. Switzerland.

Welbers, K., Koniin, E. A., Burgers, C., de Vaate, A. B., Edison, A., & Brugman, B. C. (2019). Gamification as a tool for engaging student learning: A field experiment with a gamified app. *E-learning and Digital Media, 16*(2), 92–109. doi: 10.1177/2042753018818342

Yildirim, I. (2017). The effects of gamification-based teaching practices on student achievement and students' attitudes towards lessons. *The Internet and Higher Education, 33*, 86–92. doi: 10.1016/j.iheduc.2017.02.002

Young, M. F., Slota, S., Cuter, A. B., Jalette, G., Mulin, G., & Lai B. (2012). Our princess is in another castle: A review of trends in serious gaming for education. *Review of Educational Research, 82*(1), 61–89.

Zhiqiang, Z., Da Jun, T., Xiaoming, D., Chong, N., Choon, S., & Choe, W. (2019). *Gamification platform for manufacturing shopfloor training – A case study.* Proceedings of the 15th International CDIO Conference, Aarhus University, Aarhus Denmark.

Chapter 7

Augmented Reality Apps: A Developer's Perception

R. Balaji

Sree Ramakrishna College of Engineering, Coimbatore, India

Contents

DOI: 10.1201/9781003175896-7

7.1 Introduction

The industrial revolution is considered to be one of the important factors that not only has a direct impact on the national economy but also has an indirect global impact. Globally, there has been so much improvement in the field of technology use, added to the fact that technology development is accelerating exponentially. From the mechanization of stream engines in 1700 AD to the present solar-powered vehicles, technology has improved to a great extent, reducing carbon emissions and the hazards posed to human lives and increasing productivity. As we enter into the 21st century, the age of millennials, technology has improved from being a mechanical and workforce-based stream to a digitalized one. This century has just witnessed the next shift in the Industrial Revolution phase, or "Industry 4.0". This includes major emerging technologies like artificial intelligence and machine learning, automation and robotics, big data, Internet of Things, cyber security, blockchain, cloud computing, mobile applications, and augmented reality (AR) and virtual reality (VR). This work describes an introduction to AR, general use cases, the technology stack that can be readily adapted, an overview of how to get started, a small comparison of the trend of AR in the world with that of India, and finally a small application that can be run on a mobile device. This is a simple app that illustrates the basic functionality of AR.

7.2 What is AR?

The term "augmented reality" was coined by a researcher, Thomas Caudell, at Boeing Company, which is primarily an aerospace manufacturing industry, in the year 1990. Although there are many speculations related to the theory that the work had already begun back in 1969 at Harvard University, the real prototype was developed by Mr. Caudell. The prototype that was developed was made to facilitate the pilots of the Boeing aircraft to have visual data about their aircraft's complex wiring schematics. But, unlike modern days, where an AR device is compact and lightweight, it weighed hundreds of kilograms and had to be mounted on the ceiling. The user interface was not well developed. All that the user was can able to do was to visually interpret what was going on in the aircraft.

The second issue was the amount of power it consumed. All these factors made it practically impossible to be fitted on planes back in those days. But, it was very valuable because it could be used for training pilots on the ground level. As said by various personalities, "There is always a small step towards a massive invention" – it sparked the first development in the field of AR and VR. From the year 1992, there has been so much research and development in the field of AR and VR, and in recent times, its scope has extended well beyond what was estimated in the early 1990s. The use cases, as well as the technological stack involved in the field of AR, have exponentially grown owing to its complexity. AR now comes as a feature in most smartphones. As the trend towards AR increases day by day, many Fortune 100 company like Google, Microsoft, Apple, Facebook, etc., have started to dedicate a piece of their resources to AR research and development (R&D), with one goal to create a more cost-effective and efficient product. From all the above factors, it's evident that AR is going to be one of the key contributors, not only in present times but also in future days to come.

7.3 AR/VR – The Big Picture

As the name "AR/VR" is complicated to pronounce, even the simplest meaning tends to be one of the confusing topics that one can grasp. There is often a misconception about the two terms "augmented reality" and "virtual reality". For a developer, it might sound like an easy topic, but for a layman, it's not so. AR uses the principle of superposition of how an object would look in a real-time environment. In other terms, AR differs from VR in the sense that AR is part of the surrounding environment; it is actually "real" and just adding layers of virtual objects to the real environment. For VR, the user will be made to immerse in a virtual environment that has no connection with the real-world space, apart from the fact that the user is standing in the real-world space. In a nutshell, the user's visual perspective is locked to the virtual world and has no connection with the real world. In simpler terms, the output that AR delivers is, with reference to the real-world, like that of the user's living room, etc., whereas in VR, the output produced or delivered is with reference to a virtual world, say, for example, riding a roller coaster while sitting at home.

7.4 Augmented Reality Powered Devices

AR can be described as a piece of software that does a task based on user input or user desire like placing a virtual object on a table, floor, etc. But like all the other software, it needs some hardware to perform. This hardware comes in two main forms:

1. Smartphones
2. Head-mounted Displays

Smartphones are one of the most common personal gadgets that are found these days, so developers often make applications for mobile phones. On the other hand, not all smartphones that are readily available on market can be used for this purpose. Developers can opt to make apps for lightweight models so that the application can run on almost all devices. But, the extendibility, scalability, and features that one can expect out of lightweight models are in question, and these are less than most developers would opt for when developing an app. The main reasons that contribute to this drawback can be listed as follows:

1. Compatibility
2. Performance
3. Hardware Specifications

Compatibility is one of the important factors while building any application. Recent trends show that the smartphone market is evolving at a constant rate. Another study shows that older users hesitate to buy a new smartphone, especially in India. This leaves developers with a gap in choosing which level to develop an app for. The second factor is performance; usually performance and hardware specifications are inter-relatable. With higher hardware specifications, an AR app can perform very well, but this comes with a higher price tag for the mobile phone. The main reason is that, just as the AR app starts functioning, it draws more computational power.

The head-mounted display is another type of AR device that can outperform traditional smartphone-based AR. The main reason is the number of sensors encapsulated or fitted inside it. The main factor that restricts developers is the huge cost. In India, a basic head-mounted headset normally costs at least $50,000. One of the notable manufacturers is Microsoft HoloLens. Google also makes Google Glass, but it is not as popular as the one produced by Microsoft.

7.5 Rules and Constraints to be Followed

As for every product, be it software or hardware, AR has certain rules or constraints that have to be considered when developing an app. Some of them are as follows.

7.5.1 Placing

When an object is anchored, or "placed" in simple terms, it should be able to be placed on any flat surface like a wall, ceiling, or even mid-air. The object should behave the same way as real-world objects would behave. This forms the basic rule for any AR application.

7.5.2 Scaling and Size

When placed, AR should change size and dimension relative to the device. This is made possible based on an understanding of the real world.

7.5.3 Occlusion

Occlusion is a phenomenon that happens to an image or object that is blocked by another real-world object. This is the most important part of any AR principle and is considered one of the tricky aspects of AR.

7.5.4 Lighting, Solid Assets, and Context Awareness

These factors are the secondary factors that are considered when building a realistic application. An animation should act accordingly whenever there is a change in lighting in a room, etc.

7.5.5 Tracking

AR archives hardware and software realism in two major tracking ways. This is also one of the key factors in determining the design aesthetics of an AR device. They are as follows:

1. Inside-Out Tracking
2. Outside-In Tracking

Inside-out tracking means that all the sensors, error measurements, and rectification units are built in the device itself. The best examples are mobile phones and head-mounted devices. The advantage of this method is the simplicity of the process. The cons are that limited resources will be spent on rendering, processing, and unrealistic visualization of the data thus processed. In contrast, outside-in tracking makes use of external sensors, processors like graphical processing units (GPUs). We can configure the processing of the rendering, and more advanced processes like that of procedural generation, which is limited in the case of inside-out tracking, but it comes with a huge price tag.

7.5.6 Anchors

Anchors are the assets or the object placed in the AR. These are the essential aspects of AR. Anchors can also be defined as user-defined points in the space, which are already defined by a process called plane detection.

7.6 Augmented Reality Libraries

The rules that were mentioned in the previous part might sound overwhelming for a person who might be new to AR development. It is often a more challenging concept even for developers to explicitly consider all the rules and thus framing an app. To ease the process of development and also, running an app based on a specific requirement with a common platform, many tech giants like Google (Google Developers, 2021), and Apple (Apple Inc., 2021), made several of Library will ease in production. There a few libraries which are mostly open-source, but there are also subscription-based libraries. The two widely famous open-source libraries are

1. ARCore
2. ARKit

ARCore is an open-source platform or, in other words, a framework library that supports AR development, for both Android and iOS, whereas ARKit, published by Apple, is an open-source framework that supports only Apple devices running on iOS and is required for AR content to be delivered. The main reason that ARKit is not available for Android devices is hardware dependency. The platform requires A-series processors like A13-bionic chips, released a few months back, and also depends on the depth camera feature, which are not available on Android phones. But ARCore is seen pushing limits in some of the flagship phones, like those manufactured by reputed smartphone manufacturing companies like Samsung, OnePlus, Vivo, Xiaomi, etc., to match up with Apple's ARKit. Currently, ARCore supports plane detection, basic occlusion, point cloud, lighting estimation, marker and markerless detection, and finally cloud anchors. ARKit supports the same things as ARCore, but it extends to supporting face detection, shared world, and people occlusion. But unlike developing other Android apps through various platforms like Android Studio or MIT App Inventor, or developing an iOS app through XCode, an AR app cannot be easily built using these platforms. The reason is that AR consists of a 3D frame of reference, and it requires a game engine like Unity 3D, which will help developers to visualize and create apps in real time. Unity 3D is a game engine developed by Unity Technologies (2021), mainly to develop 2D and 3D games, which was later adopted by AR enthusiasts in developing AR apps. The main advantage of Unity 3D is that the programmer does not have to program how a 3D model of his perception should act as a C #Script. By invoking the Android SDK that is available through Android Studio, or as an XCode for Apple devices, Unity 3D builds, runs, and creates a Gradle project and thereby creates an .apk or .ipa file and also helps to debug the code. This work focuses entirely on Android-based phones and AR applications developed using ARCore.

Apart from ARCore and ARKit, there are a few other AR-based libraries or framework platforms like Vuforia Augmented Reality Support, which is free but requires a subscription if the usage exceeds certain queries.

Now, from the context, it is seen that either ARCore or ARKit is an essential part of creating an AR application. However, all these frameworks could only implement certain methods. For a more interactive experience, Unity published a framework called ARFoundation, which will allow users to create an interactive AR experience. ARFoundation allows developers to work with AR platforms in a multi-platform way within Unity. By invoking these packages from Unity Package Manager, it is possible to seamlessly connect a framework like ARCore with the hardware of the device being used. But, ARFoundation requires ARKit Plugin or ARCore Plugin to work in order to target a specific AR platform.

ARFoundation allows developers to create AR apps that work on the widest possible range of smartphones by creating a common AR API and a set of AR components that work in conjunction with either ARCore or ARKit as the smartphone AR layer. Because ARFoundation is built on the core AR capabilities common to both platforms, it is based on the most stable or solid AR capabilities.

7.7 Hardware ARCore Correlation

ARCore depends on many hardware components to make AR a dream come true. The main reason is that any AR app requires being aware of its surrounding, which is not possible only by a camera turning around. The concept of computer vision is possible but restricted by key components like computation power. Because of this reason, AR depends on numerous sensors and hardware that will provide input to the system. It can broadly be classified into two major sub-categories:

1. Motion Tracking
2. Location-Based AR Services

The key hardware or sensors for motion tracking are camera, gyroscope, accelerometer and magnetometer, and GPS for location-based AR services. In addition to this, a light proximity sensor is used for assessing global light falling on an object, through which we can change the way an object reacts when placed in a well-lit environment.

Accelerometer: measures acceleration, which is a change in speed divided by time. In simple words, it's the measure of change in velocity. Acceleration forces can be static like gravity or continuous, such as movement or vibrations.

Gyroscope: measures and maintains orientation and angular velocity. When there is a change in rotation of the phone while using an AR experience, the gyroscope measures that rotation, and ARCore ensures that the digital assets respond correctly.

Phone Camera: with mobile AR, the phone camera supplies a live feed of the surrounding real world upon which AR content is overlaid. In addition to the camera itself, ARCore-capable phones like the Google Pixel rely on complementary technologies like machine learning, complex image processing, and computer vision to produce high-quality images and spatial maps for mobile AR.

Magnetometer: gives smartphones a simple orientation related to the Earth's magnetic field. Because of the magnetometer, the phone always knows which direction is north, allowing it to auto-rotate digital maps depending on the physical orientation. This device is key to location-based AR apps.

GPS: a global navigation satellite system that provides geolocation data and time information to a GPS receiver, like in the smartphone. For ARCore-capable smartphones, this device helps enable location-based AR apps, which is possible through Android Studio only because there is no known open-source software development kit (SDK).

7.8 Mapping and Other Key Concepts

Now, the inputs having been obtained, the ARCore, in simpler terms, starts to create a map of the data obtained primarily from the camera of the device and from other inputs like the magnetometer, gyroscope, etc. This becomes the data, and three main processes take place, which serve as the backbone of the entire AR app to have a memory of what has been encountered so far. The key processes are as follows:

1. Motion Tracking
2. Environmental Understanding
3. Anchors

AR platforms need to know when the phone is been moved. The general technology behind this is called simultaneous localization and mapping, or SLAM. This is the process by which smartphones analyze, understand, and orient themselves to the physical world. SLAM processes require data-collecting hardware like cameras, depth sensors, light sensors, gyroscopes, and accelerometers. ARCore uses all of these to create an understanding of the environment and uses that information to correctly render augmented experiences by detecting planes and feature points to set appropriate anchors. Apart from various techniques like visual odometry, computer vision, and video tracking, ARCore uses a process called concurrent odometry and mapping, or COM, which means that COM tells a smartphone where it's located in space in relationship to the world around it. It does this by capturing visually distinct features in the environment, which are called feature points.

Environmental understanding is ARCore's process for seeing, processing, and using information about the physical world around an AR device. The process begins with feature points. The same feature points are used for motion tracking. ARCore uses your phone's camera to capture clusters of feature points along a surface to create what's known as a plane. "Plane finding" is the term for ARCore's ability to detect and generate flat surfaces. ARCore's awareness of these planes is what allows it to properly place and adjust 3D assets in physical space, such as on the floor or on a table. Otherwise, objects would just float. This process enables you to do things like see how a plant would look on your desk. Once you know where the planes in the world are, you can hit "test" or "ray cast" to see what plane you are tapping on. This allows you to place objects on top of the floor or on the ceiling and so on.

Finally, the anchors, as seen before, are user-defined points that will allow the solid 3D virtual objects (assets) to get placed on the detected plane surfaces.

7.9 Use Cases

Some of the well-known use cases in the field of AR are as follows:

1. Social Media
2. Gaming
3. Education
4. Healthcare
5. Shopping and Business

7.9.1 Social Media

Various social media platforms like Instagram and Snapchat have incorporated AR-based face filters using a technique called face mesh, which enables users to seamlessly have a filter anchored to their face. The filters may be a crown made out of flowers, a bee-like face, and so on.

7.9.2 Gaming

AR-based gaming is yet to be explored by the community, but it's worth noting that it is estimated that AR-based games should come to mainframe mobile-based games in the year 2022.

7.9.3 Education

AR in education is the place where I hold my expertise. The main goal is to reduce the concept of "mugging-up", a rote learning with no permanent base in memory which is prevalent in school children. AR in education consists of 3D models or animations played in any text/content in a textbook published by various reputed textbook manufactures. The 3D models or animations that will be used will be realistic so that the user, in this case, the students, will gather in-depth knowledge about what it looks like in the real world in 3D instead of the traditional 2D frame of reference.

7.9.4 Healthcare

Healthcare has seen increased AR-based training for staff and doctors in how to treat patients in real time without explicitly operating or studying on patients. This is more prevalent in developed countries like the United States, Germany, Britain, Russia, etc., and is yet to be practiced in a country like India.

7.9.5 Shopping and Business

Shopping has been the forefront application of AR. The reason is that the user can place objects like furniture, appliances, etc., in real time in their homes and can view how the items will look in real time without spending money. One of the major adopters of this method in their business was IKEA, a major furniture manufacturer in the United States. Another application is virtual try-ons of various clothing accessories like shirts, gowns, etc., which has been implemented by various multinational fashion brands. The best example of AR-based shopping in India is a glasses company called SpecMakers. They were the first company to successfully implement AR-based shopping through their website in India.

7.10 Development of a Simple Augmented Reality Application

Now, we'll try to build a simple but effective no-code program that will illustrate an AR application in real time on an Android phone, which consists of ARCore, or an Apple device that is capable of running ARKit. By following along with this documentation, you can understand the basics of Unity 3D engine, its overall outlook, setup, and initialization of the development environment.

7.10.1 Downloading Unity

To download Unity, please refer to the link (https://unity3d.com/get-unity/download) that is given for proper downloading and installation of Unity Hub (Figure 7.1).

Users must be signed into their accounts to download further versions of Unity 3D editors. If users are not signed in, they might need to redo the process, which is explained in the documentation provided by Unity. First, download and install Unity Hub from the given link, which will allow you to download the specific version of Unity Editor. After this installation, open Unity Hub -> Installs -> Add

Figure 7.1 Unity Download (Unity Technologies, 2020).

-> Choose Which Version and Dependencies you'll be requiring. Click on Next -> Finish (Figure 7.2)

This download process takes a few moments depending upon the network speed and bandwidth, and it will also install many other dependencies such as

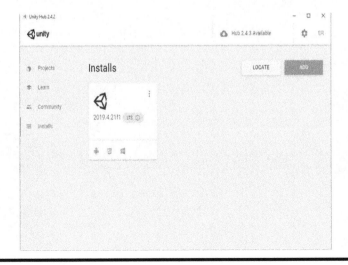

Figure 7.2 Unity Hub.

visual studio and libraries. This is the first and foremost step for the setup and installation of any project.

7.10.2 Creating a New Project and Working around It

After successful installation of Unity, you might need to start a new project, which is accessible through the Unity Hub. After completion of this process, you should be able to start working with the Unity Editor. Some of the basic requirements that need to be fulfilled after the initialization of the project are as follows:

1. To change the environment from PC to Android, go to File -> Build Settings -> Change to Android and click Switch Platform (Figure 7.3).
2. To change company name and product name, go to File -> Build Settings -> Player Settings -> Company Name & Product Name (Figure 7.4).
3. To set the minimum and maximum Android compatibility versions, go to File -> Build Settings -> Player Settings -> Other Settings -> Minimum API Level & Target API Level (Figure 7.5).
4. To integrate Android Studio SDK and Android Studio JDK with Unity, go to Edit -> Preference -> External Tools -> Android JDK & Android SDK (Figure 7.6).

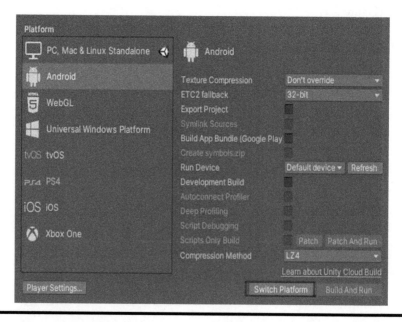

Figure 7.3   Change Platform.

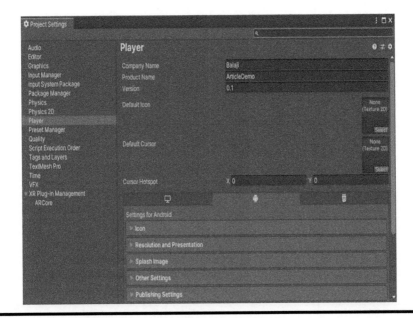

Figure 7.4   Change Company and Product Name.

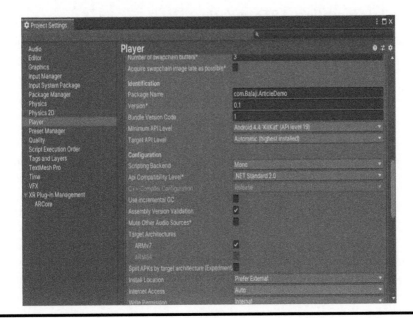

Figure 7.5   Target API.

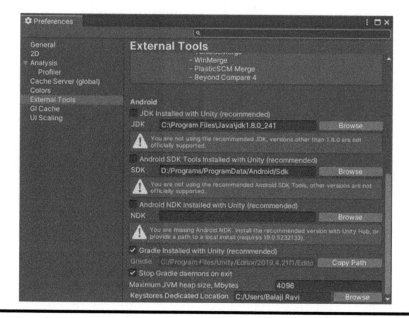

Figure 7.6   Setup JDK, SDK.

7.10.3 Integrating ARFoundation

To work with a foundation, first we need to initialize setting libraries, which will indirectly allow us to enable an AR-based workflow in our application. To do this, go to the Windows toolbar inside the Unity Editor, and select Package Manager. We'll need some of the packages that are listed below (Figure 7.7):

1. ARFoundation
2. XR management
3. **ARCore XR plugin** (If you are using an Android-based development environment or **ARKit XR plugin** if you are working in an iOS-based development environment)
4. **XR interaction toolkit** (This will be inside preview packages inside the Advanced tab.)

This is the end of importing various libraries that will serve as the backbone for the application. After successful importing of the libraries, close the package manager and create a new Unity scene.

7.10.4 Working with ARFoundation

With the new scene created in our workspace, the first step is to delete the main camera from the hierarchy workspace. This is done because XRToolkit has a

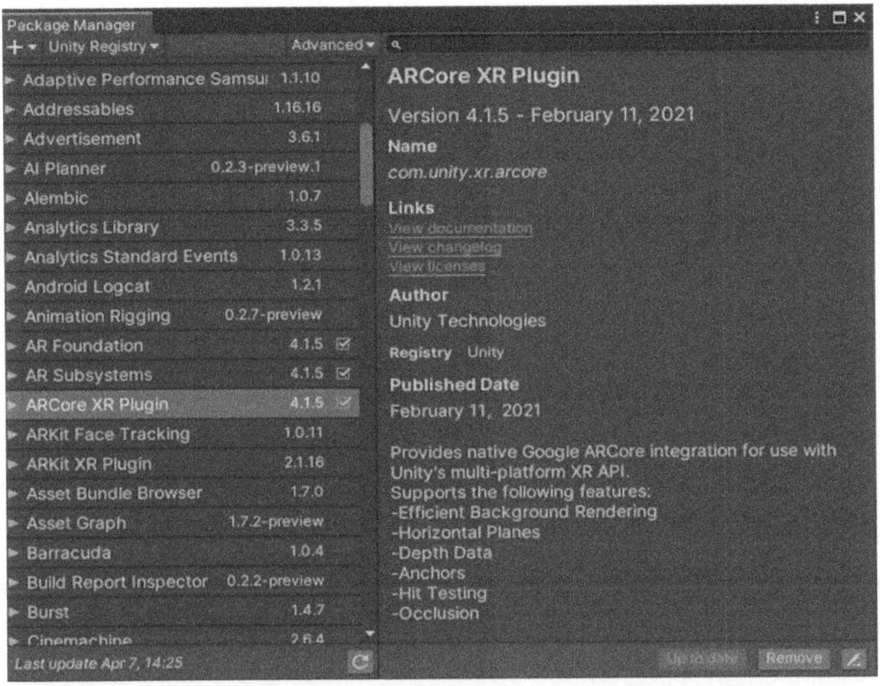

Figure 7.7 Package Manager.

default camera that will interfere with normal operation. If the main camera is not deleted, when the device is running another application, the device will use a camera to derive its position and rotation. If the normal main camera is used, the camera is referenced to an arbitrary position inside Unity Scene. Normally, it should be referenced to a position relative to the result needed to be an outcome. This is why we use ARSessionCamera, which makes the camera relative to the result. After deleting the main camera in the hierarchy window, right-click XR -> AR Session Origin (Figure 7.8).

AR session origin contains a default AR camera that will act as the main camera for our application. Make this the main camera by selecting this and going into Inspector Tab -> Tag -> MainCamera (Figure 7.9).

The next step is to instantiate the AR session. This can be done using AR Session Instance. To do this in the hierarchy window, right-click XR -> AR Session.

The next step is to convert the input that is being published by the user to the application. This can be done using an instance called AR Gesture Interactor. This can be imported through the hierarchy window; right-click XR -> AR Gesture Interactor. AR Gesture Interactor is an instance of the XR Interaction Toolkit. This instance is used to translate gestures, such as place, select, translate, rotate, and

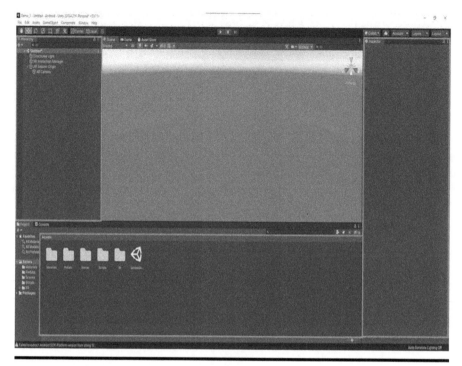

Figure 7.8   Unity Editor Different Windows.

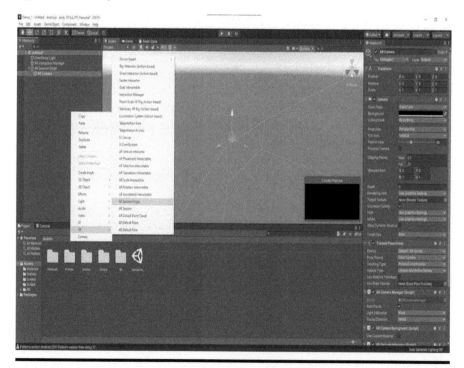

Figure 7.9   Accessing Hierarchy Window.

scale, which are given as input by the user, into object manipulation. After creating this instance, let us create another instance called AR Placement Intractable. This is an instance that will assist with the AR Gesture Interactor in making the process of development easier. This can be imported through the hierarchy window; right-click XR -> AR Placement Intractable.

Now, with all the prerequisites done, let us create an object that will allow us to visualize what we are trying to do. For this example, we'll stick to a basic example, and we'll create a cube. Creation of a cube can be done through the hierarchy window; right-click 3D -> Cube. This cube must be made in such a way that it can be available in any place other than the hierarchy window. To do this, go to Project Window -> Create a new folder. Drag the cube from the hierarchy window to this folder. This process gives us an output called a prefab. In general terms, it can be called Cube Prefab since we have made a cube as a prefab.

Now that the prefab has been created successfully, we'll assign this prefab to our application so that we can work with it. For this part, go to the hierarchy window and select AR Placement Intractable -> Inside Inspector Window. Drag and drop the Cube Prefab that was created previously to Placement Prefab Box inside AR Placement Intractable.

Now, the prefab has been created. To visualize this in real time, we need to place the cube in any plane. This can be created using a GameObject. GameObject can be considered a container, and this GameObject can consist of many other objects associated with it. To create a new GameObject, in the hierarchy window right-click Create Empty. After creating, select the created GameObject, and on the inspector window right-click Add Component -> Select AR Plane, AR Plane Mesh Visualizer, Mesh Filter, Line Render & Mesh Render. Now, we'll add some color to this mesh, which can be done using new materials. Create new materials inside the project window; right-click Material. Double-click on the material, and change the color of it from the inspector window. After selecting a suitable color, from the hierarchy window, select GameObject. Then, drag and drop the material created to mesh render of the GameObject. Do the same for the line render component also. For the line render, change the width by double-clicking on the width, and change the value to 0.005. Unselect Use World Space. Now, the visualizer has been created; make it a prefab by following the previous steps. Drag and drop the prefab created to AR Session Origin -> AR Plane Manager Component.

7.10.5 Building and Installing the Application

Now, it is time to build, compile, and run the basic application on your device. To do so, go to File -> Build Settings, and click on Add Open Scenes -> Build. The build process might take some time depending on the hardware configuration of the system. After the build process is done, an APK file will be generated, which, when installed on your phone, will allow you to enjoy a small demo application on the device.

7.11 Conclusion

The above information explains various misconceptions and other concepts that involve the use cases, rules, and popular libraries that will serve as a helping hand in developing an AR app from a developer's perspective.

References and Other Resources

Apple Inc., https://developer.apple.com/augmented-reality/arkit 25 Aug 2021. Aug 2020.

Google Developers, https://developers.google.com/ar, 25 Aug 2021.

Unity Technologies, https://docs.unity3d.com/Packages/com.unity.xr.arfoundation@2.2/manual/index.html 9 Sep 2021.

Unity technologies, https://store.unity.com/download-nuo#game-ready-templates 25 Aug 2021.

Chapter 8

Modernized Healthcare Using Augmented Reality

N.S. Sukanya[1], D. Kalaivani[2], and P. Ranjit Jeba Thangaiah[3]

[1]*Assistant Professor, School of Science Studies, CMR University, Bengaluru, India*
[2]*Associate Professor, Department of ISE, New Horizon College of Engineering, Autonomous College Permanently Affiliated to VTU, Bengaluru, India*
[3]*Associate Professor and Head, Department of Information Technology, Karunya Institute of Technology and Sciences, Coimbatore, India*

Contents

DOI: 10.1201/9781003175896-8

Objectives

This chapter addresses the following objectives:

1. Transformation of augmented reality (AR) in the healthcare discipline
2. AR applications in healthcare
3. Case studies on medical education, nurse training, dentistry, surgical visualization, and diagnostic imaging
4. Technology behind AR gadgets and software packages in application advancement

---

8.1 Introduction

The heritage of healthcare and medical science in India is rich and centuries old with holistic treatment. The modern medical systems were recognized in the 17th century, and the growth was steady. The healthcare sector is estimated to attain US$ 372 billion in the next two years. The hospital sector is estimated to reach US$ 132 billion in the next three years. The market size of the medical tourism sector is US$ 3 billion and will probably reach US$ 8 billion by 2020. The market size of the diagnostics sector is around US$ 4 billion.[1] In recent times, augmented reality (AR) has attained influence among healthcare professionals for several approaches such as diagnostic procedures, surgical preparation, medical training, and drug discovery.

Information technology companies are venturing into this sector to apply AR technology for assisting medical professionals to ease diagnostic and treatment procedures. AR applications aid the patients by educating them to get acquainted with the basic healthcare information, to cooperate with doctors to analyze the surgical procedures, and to undergo painless medical procedures.

An interactive web-based portal for AR assists users to experience a real environment by covering digital aspects in the real world. Currently, there are several AR healthcare applications available. The AR healthcare market is categorized by product, technology, end-user, and region. AR products use display devices, cameras, input devices, and sensors. AR technology uses handheld and head-mounted devices. AR end-users are research laboratories, hospitals, and diagnostics hubs. The region-wise AR market is analyzed across Asia, Europe, and North America.

The influence of COVID-19 in the AR healthcare market has observed significant growth in surgical procedures. Three-dimensional (3D) visualizing of the internal organs aids the surgeons in obtaining a real view during the surgery. AccuVein is an AR device used to visualize the veins in the human body for injections. This device eases the blood drawing and injection process for medical professionals and subsequently reduces vein punctures for patients.[2]

Many hospitals lack quality service due to insufficient staff, provide limited care towards patients, and lack advanced equipment, which leads to inefficient healthcare in hospitals. The use of interactive visualizing applications in healthcare provides an enriching experience to medical professionals and patients. Patients are at ease during medical procedures. AR uses virtual components in the physical environment to synchronize with the natural world. AR can become a learning tool in medical education. It provides a better understanding while working jointly with virtual items and real environments. Also, it provides decision making, teamwork, and creative learning experiences (Zhu, Hadadgar, Masiello, & Zary, 2014). AR-integrated simulation teaching is a conceptual model introduced by Carlson and Gagnon (2016) in healthcare education to combine AR with simulation concepts and game theory. The trials of integrated simulation indicate that the pattern can be adapted to other disciplines.

In 1990, the term "augmented reality" was created by Tom and David (Carmigniani et al., 2011), and the first head-mounted AR display was invented to aid aircraft workers in the wiring process. In 1992, an advanced AR system was created named "Virtual Fixtures".[3] In 1994, AR was used in the theater and entertainment industries to project virtual objects on stage.[3] In 1998, a live NFL game was broadcasted while displaying virtual yellow lines and other graphics.[3] In 1999, NASA created a spacecraft using a hybrid synthetic vision system.[3] Later, in 2000, the first AR game was built, and many AR applications were developed in other disciplines, such as the medical field, tourism, marketing, fashion, entertainment, and travel (Berryman, 2012). In 2009, AR was used in print media to create Pages Alive.[3] In 2013, the automotive industry used AR for technical assistance by providing repair instructions.[3] In 2014, wearable AR technology was introduced, such as Google Glass, for various applications.[3] In 2016, advanced wearable AR technology named HoloLens was created to scan the surroundings.[3] In 2017, the retail industry used AR to allow customers to preview products before making a purchase.[3] There was a record growth in training and teaching, consumer entertainment, social media, and voice assistance in autonomous cars.

There are so many challenges while adopting AR in the healthcare industry. Funding for research, product development, and marketing are the major monetary issues. The next category of the issue is the technical limitations, such as the size of the VR system, computer specifications, and the resolution of the devices.

Also, there exist organizational issues in the hospitals to adapt to the modern technology, deficiency of knowledge with the patients and the end-users, and lack of adequate research studies in AR healthcare. Regulations, policies, markets, lack of interest, insurance, and anxiety about the side effects are the other issues to consider. Hence, extensive research is going on in the AR healthcare industry to identify and overcome the hardship in executing AR-based applications in the medical field. There is a necessity to evaluate and validate AR-based applications in healthcare to conquer this hardship. This chapter discusses the history, applications, latest technology, benefits, and limitations of AR, as well as future outlooks in the healthcare industry.

8.2 AR Applications in Healthcare

AR applications are prevalent in the healthcare sector. In the medical discipline, AR is likely to see remarkable growth. AR specialty areas in medical training are surgery, forensics, anatomy, laparoscopic surgery, and anesthesia. A virtual interactive environment is constructed such as a surgical site, a surgical room, therapeutic imitation, and patient anatomy. The productiveness of AR in medical training was studied with the help of the Google Glass simulation application (Herron, 2016). AR operation is one of the renowned areas where the surgeon positions the patient's scan area above the body digitally by wearing a mask. This is an add-on tool to assist surgeons in finding the issues that were missed during diagnostics. Brain surgery is done with the aid of AR since the area is sensitive to a huge number of arteries and mild tissues. Surgeons use wearable devices so that AR applications overlay the scan reports of patients over their actual bodies; surgeons then understand how to proceed with the surgery.[4]

Open surgery with the support of AR is a challenging procedure where surgeons can visualize the internal organs in 3D representation, virtually. Open surgery is accomplished by evaluating real and simulated data sources through visualization. Studies revealed that only one in-vitro experiment out of thirteen experiments was completed, and the remaining studies were executed in clinical settings (Fida, Cutolo, di Franco, Ferrari, & Ferrari, 2018). AR usage relies on the surgical skills and intellect of surgeons. A miniature device to overlay the image, which is a 3D projection, assists the surgeons in a precise examination of the structure of the patient's body (Gavaghan, Peterhans, Oliveira-Santos, & Weber, 2011). Image-directed surgery with robot assistance has been performed, especially for critical surgeries. AR technology provides the surgeons with an enhanced view, improved control over the vascular structure, and tool actions such as inserting, rotating, and pulling (Kobayashi, Zhang, Collins, Karim, & Merck, 2018).

During the surgery using an AR system, computer-processed image data is given to the surgeons in actual time through hardware and software. With the help of video cameras, projectors, trackers, electronic display devices, and other

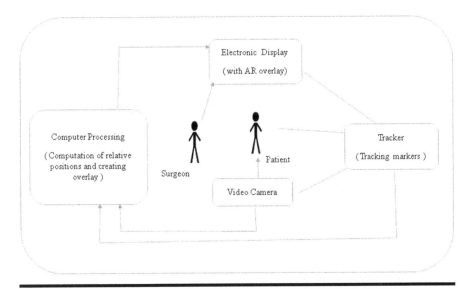

Figure 8.1 Elementary AR Principles During a Surgery.

customized equipment, AR is projected. The basic technique is to overlay a computer graphics image on a real-time image caught by a video camera and display it by combining these images using a projector. The benefit of the AR system is that it does not demand surgeons to turn away from the surgery, unlike conventional visualization practices (Figure 8.1).

8.2.1 AR in Surgery

In surgeries related to the removal of malignant tissues from healthy tissues, images guide the surgery, and surgeons use Near InfraRed Fluorescence (NIRF). It provides information dynamically to surgeons during surgery. With the NIRF imaging technique and display system, surgeons can locate the malignant tissues that have to be snipped out and preserve the healthy tissues. Suitable NIRF systems with HoloLens technology minimize the imaging impression and operational cost. The surgeon's vision is replaced with an AR view, which is the limitation of this technology. With the assistance of HoloLens, the NIRF image is captured with a high-quantity sensor that has a laser light source. The NIRF image is transformed into a hologram that is viewed on HoloLens and aligned with the surgeons' natural eyesight (Cui, Kharel, & Gruev, 2017). Amini and Kersten-Oertel (2019) came up with an AR application, where surgeons can view the outline of implants using 3D holograms. The AR system prototype was developed using HoloLens for mastectomy procedures. The authors developed a dual-chamber implant to view individual forms, and the system was tested using 13 substances. The actual and holographic implants were compared to decide which could be used. This technique was more accurate and user friendly than the conventional technique. The system was evaluated to identify the minor variations in the shapes of various hologram implants and match them with the actual shape.

Sirilak and Muneesawang (2018) developed a prototype model for remote consultation using an AR holographic system in an intensive care unit specifically in rural areas to provide extraordinary quality medical services to critical patients through advanced HoloLens devices. A communicating platform is created for remote consulting, which addresses the gap in rural areas where there is a deficiency of dedicated equipment and medical specialists. The analysis shows that applying HoloLens devices is reliable in remote consulting in rural areas. The "Proximie" healthcare app remotely connects two doctors to interact during a surgery. A skilled surgeon from a remote location can view the operation with the help of a live video from the operation theater. The AR app serves as an interface for live streaming between the two doctors for efficient interaction.[5]

8.2.2 AR System for Diagnosis

The arrangement of veins can be viewed on the skin's surface with the help of an AR display system. The "AccuVein" app uses a portable scanning device to identify veins. The collaboration between the laser beam and the hemoglobin in the blood visualizes the veins of a patient by spotlighting only the veins. It is a challenge for doctors and nurses to understand the veins by looking at them with the naked eye when the patient under observation is an infant, an older adult, or a person with dark-colored skin. AccuVein eliminates the patient's discomfort by providing an efficient solution. VeinSeekPro AR app works in iOS, and VeinSeek AR app works in the Android platform. Just install the AR app on a mobile phone and identify the veins. It uses a mobile phone camera and flashlight for vein visualization.[5]

Vivarra's dental app is available for Android and iOS platforms to teach patients about teeth care. It is specially designed for kids to experience the waiting room in a dental clinic. Another AR system aids dentists to view 3D images, by scanning the patient's mouth and identifying dental problems. A head-mounted device such as AR glasses enables dentists to view an infected tooth and analyze the depth of the cavity. This provides the dentist with details regarding the region to drill the tooth if the dentist wants to by reducing the uneasiness of the patient. The AR system software aids the dentist in extracting teeth and other dental procedures such as tooth implants and designing crowns. Dentists use 3D virtual models to train dental graduates and assistants by allowing them to experience and examine numerous categories of dental problems and provide solutions.[6]

8.2.3 AR in Pharmaceuticals

AR is taking the pharmaceutical industry to the next stage, and the growth is tremendous. The scientific developments in drug discovery have to be

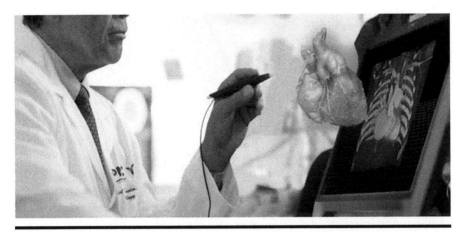

Figure 8.2   A 3D Animated Image that Hovers When Pointed by an AR-Enabled Device.

implemented exactly to attain the integrity of a pharmaceutical product. Even a slight inaccuracy will lead to an unproductive treatment or produce adverse re-actions, and it is unacceptable to produce that drug. The AR system removes human errors and brings quality to the pharmaceutical product. In pharmaceutical marketing, AR is applied to showcase the integrity of the new drug to buyers. A 3D visualization of an organ can be provided to show how a specific medicine works in the human body. The advanced AR approach is an efficient tool to introduce various products to customers. The digital interaction using AR shows the effi-ciency of a novel product and encourages buyers by showing the difference from the traditional treatment methods. 3D medical animations fly off the screen by pointing the mobile device at the drug.[7] Figure 8.2 shows a 3D animated image that hovers when the AR-enabled device points at it.

8.2.4 Medical Training Using AR

"Touch Surgery" is an AR app to learn surgical procedures by performing virtual surgery through simulators. The app is available on Android and iOS platforms. The 3D interface is effortless to practice and is interactive during touch operation. The app is connected to an oversized database consisting of nearly 150 simulations for different surgeries. To learn about the anatomy of the human body, there is an app for AR clothes that is user-friendly and provides a fun learning experience for kids. A printed code on a T-shirt, identified by the AR app, gives a realistic scene of the internal organs of a real person. The healthcare app promotes health con-sciousness, self-help, medical services, and courses. These apps help students vi-sualize the human body quicker and make learning easier to understand, thereby increasing practical knowledge.[8] AR apps are used for hospital navigation to aid medical professionals to rapidly find the right room and components during emergencies. The app helps medical professionals to navigate inside the hospital during hurried scenarios. In addition, patients can change doctor appointments and locate doctor's offices through an app.[8]

8.2.5 Doctor–Patient Interaction Using an AR System

PatientAR is an AR app developed to improve doctor–patient interaction, especially for orthopaedics. It is user-friendly for both patients and doctors to view the medical treatment plan visually and understand the benefits and the risks. This AR app serves as an exact learning tool to educate both patients and doctors.

The tool collects patient data and creates case studies that give a learning experience for doctors across the globe. The information accumulated in the app aids engineers and scientists in developing an efficient product.[9] The patient interacts with the doctor through the AR app, which aids the doctors to understand the intensity of the patient's pain. The patient's attention is distracted in the virtual world, which enhances the patient's pain tolerance. The pain anxiety and chronic and acute pain are minimized, and the pain threshold is measurable in the AR app. AR plays a vital aspect in the therapy of psychological states such as phobias, autism, and short attention span. The interactive environment between the healer and the patient helps the psychologist to locate the source and limit the patient's anxiety. Telemedicine is yet another AR application where medical information is transmitted and patient care is provided from a distant location. The operator can interact with diagnostic devices, such as ultrasound, remaining in the remote location. The interactive interface creates a sensibility of physical presence for doctors and patients.[9]

8.3 AR Technologies in the Healthcare Sector

AR has been verified to be beneficial in various areas of healthcare. Especially in surgical applications such as orthopedic, cardiology, dental, and psychiatry, where 3D imaging is required, AR efficiency is proved to be successful.

8.3.1 HoloLens and Google Glass

An AR visualization technique is proposed to locate the arrangement of bones using ultrasound optical tracking, which determines similar operational computed tomography images and creates a 3D visualization of the surgery through head-affixed display equipment. The surgery is visualized using AR-enabled HoloLens. These components simplify the eye–hand connection and improve surgical navigation (El-Hariri, Pandey, Hodgson, & Garbi, 2018). Real-time AR and wearable computing devices like Google Glass are merged in a shoulder surgical procedure. Head-anchored display equipment captures and displays images and videos at the

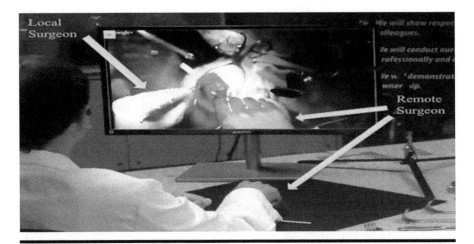

Figure 8.3   Local and Remote Surgeon Interaction Using the AR System.

same time. It works closely with the location. The local surgeon works jointly with the distant specialist existing in the surgical area virtually. The surgical results were successful; patient recovery from the shoulder pain and mobility was encouraging. Google Glass was operative in the treatment of telemedicine, such as diagnostics. The collaboration of local and remote surgeons during surgical procedures using the AR system (Ponce, Menendez, Oladeji, Fryberger, & Dantuluri, 2014) is shown below (Figure 8.3).

A smart AR system for emergency purposes was developed by combining wearable components, AR technologies, and intelligent and multi-agent systems. It portrays as a middleware named augmented field to support teams working for rescue operations. The AR system is modeled to provide services for agents exploring various enlargements and coordinate with the team in the real environment during emergency scenarios. The rescuer, being in the physical location, can work efficiently by interacting with the team positioned in the remote location (Brunetti, Croatti, Ricci, & Viroli, 2015).

AR technology is adopted in physical rejuvenation by linking AR games with wearable sensor equipment. The health of patients during physical rejuvenation is improved in the AR system.

A 3D printing method was developed using AR to create a specific tool for patients to fit in the desired location. This application software works using HoloLens, and it is verified on a 3D printed illusion imitating the patient's structure. Doctors can visualize the external and internal organs, such as skin and bones, and locate the problem area in the patient's body. The app can be put into use in surgical and training fields through simulation. Software is validated for AR head-attached display devices and other gadgets such as tablets and smartphones (Moreta-Martinez et al., 2018). This methodology was applied in a maxillofacial medical procedure (Zhu et al., 2017), where a trailing indicator was linked to the patient's mandible for AR registration. The AR method used a 3D laser printer to produce a specific tool for the patient with an automatic tracking marker, which supported registration between the factual world and AR. Additionally, the surgeons tested the tool during real surgical interference.

Image-assisted surgeries have benefits such as minimum threat of infection, quick recovery, and better pain management. Normally, the surgeon will shift the focus between the patient and the monitor in image-assisted surgeries, which is the critical drawback of it. This drawback was resolved by using images that are AR-enabled, which will assist in surgery. Vavra, P et al., (2017) conducted a review to assess the improvements in surgical procedures as a result of using Augmented Reality. The AR-enabled solution can work on mobile and desktop devices. The number of focus shifts by the physician is reduced, which leads to modernized procedures through AR visualization. Mobile-enabled image-assisted neurosurgery is performed by visualizing the AR views. Neurosurgery is performed through mobile-based AR visualization by determining the area, size, and outline of the internal part, and surgery is executed to locate the tumor (Leger, Drouin, Collins, Popa, & Kersten-Oertel, 2017).

8.3.2 Virtual Reality and Mixed Reality

Several studies in different disciplines unveil that merging the physical and computerized environment, known as mixed reality (MR), produces the outcome with high efficiency and higher precision. In plastic surgeries, the two technologies, namely virtual reality (VR) and AR, are blended in different stages of operation, such as preoperative and intraoperative stages, to obtain superior results. Many investigations were undertaken on craniofacial surgery to promote the MR methodology. In surgical education, MR renders good apprehension of the concepts to physicians. Proposals have been done for healthcare applications with MR technologies that would be both creative and novel (Sayadi et al., 2019).

Verhey, Haglin, Verhey, and Hartigan (2020) conducted a review on AR, VR, and MR applications in orthopedic surgeries. Computer-aided surgeries maximize operative exactness and safety, and minimize complications. The accuracy and precision of the surgery increases as surgeons visualize the data in real time, thereby improving treatment quality. Reality technologies offer a novel type of medical education by conducting remote mentoring and live assessments.

To upgrade the learning outcome, especially in nursing training, innovative pedagogical techniques using VR and AR systems are applied.

To enrich the diagnosis, advanced medical imaging is adapted to visually represent the intricate anatomy of the body. AR with 3D imaging delivers depth insights of the images and provides an interface for humans and the apparatus. Applying AR technology enhances the assessment in the diagnosis of breast cancer, improves the care extended to patients, and minimizes the cost (Douglas, Wilke, Gibson, Boone, & Wintermark, 2017). In AR and MR, virtual and real-world images are displayed concurrently by permitting the user to communicate in parallel. The user wears a head-fitted display unit to view virtual and real-world images. In AR, a transparent hologram-like image is viewed, and in MR a solid image is seen using HoloLens (Lovo et al., 2007).

Advanced AR technology can be utilized to personalize medicine to address the challenges of personalized therapy. AR adapts new techniques, such as eye-tracking, motion tracking, speech, and voice recognition. The influence of AR in personalized medicine can be oriented in the treatment method for image-assisted 3D surgical navigation, senior citizens, medication adherence, and addiction (Lee & Lee, 2018). MR applications are profitable in the manufacture of pharmaceuticals to transmit the experimental process across various laboratories in the world. Drug manufacturing activities involve the fusion of chemical and biological components, developing formulations, analysis, engineering, drug development, wrapping, and distribution. All the processes are vital for drug detection and growth. The influence of advancements in drug detection in the pharmaceutical industry is too complex. With the assistance of MR apps, scientists can share information rapidly using real-time systems through webcams, mobile phones, and other MR headsets, such as HoloLens, for hands-free knowledge transfers. Additionally, real-time data investigation and conversation can be performed with the researchers and vendors (Forrest et al., 2017).

8.3.3 IoT

Many AR applications are compatible with the Internet of Things (IoT), which can be accessed through smartphones. Wearable wireless devices communicate with smartphones through sensors. Once the processing is done, the data are analyzed and uploaded to the AWS cloud setting. The various technological tools like Apple ARKit and iPhone, IMU, ECG, and Simblee are utilized in various kinds of interactions in different situations based on difficulty level (Monge & Postolache, 2018).

The future of medicine is IoT. The appropriate term is the "Internet of Health (IoH)", and it refers to internet technology in the healthcare discipline (Smorodin et al., 2017). Various healthcare digital transformations are on-demand healthcare; big data in healthcare; treating patients with AR, VR, and MR; development of wearable medical equipment; predictive healthcare; and use of artificial intelligence, supercomputers, and hybrid cloud computing technologies.

8.3.4 Mirror Metaphor

Advances in AR automation have the likelihood to be used in radiological education and training. There is a great potential in the radiology department where communication with colleagues during radiological procedures, patients, and referring doctors is performed effectively (Uppot et al., 2019).

A novel magic mirror technique using an AR system is introduced to explore the anatomy of the structures. The mirror metaphor is employed in the AR system to view the reflection along with the virtual image that is overlaid on the display system. The mirror AR system is used in training for the gross anatomy course. The learning outcome of the study using the mirror AR system is compared with the course encompassing pure radiological training. The results of the mirror AR system outperform the traditional training methodology (Bork et al., 2019). The application of AR in medical imaging is an add-on to radiology training, where a 3D learning environment is built. The benefits of using AR in radiology are as follows: it has the facility to experience a 3D model of the physical environment, the facility to obtain experimental learning that will be impossible to perform in the real world, and enhanced knowledge transfer and collaboration with counterparts (Dalgarno & Lee, 2010). AR is being used to teach interventional radiology processes, to view simulation outcomes to contrast material, to coordinate use of VR glasses on smartphones, to scan an interventional radiology apparatus, to perform 3D printing, and to position the patient for diagnostic examinations in the AR environment (McCarthy, Alvin, Do, Dawson, & Uppot, 2018).

AR software is created to visualize the 3D models of the images from CT scan results. This novel technology aids doctors to study the scan results and come to a conclusion. The technology helps to take the images and divide them to examine the internal parts for surgical planning. The system is user-friendly for doctors and radiologists to work on 3D models created from CT scans (Izard, Mendez, Ruisoto, & Garcia-Penalvo, 2018).

8.3.5 Simulators

Medical simulations combined with AR applications in dental training have various advantages like practicing with dental instruments, acquiring skills quickly, and acquiring practical knowledge.

The classical applications in dentistry, using dental implant positioning, are maxillofacial and oral medical procedures (Kwon, Park, & Han, 2018). The AR application acts as an information filter by displaying the appropriate data to the surgeons during dental implant positioning (Katic et al., 2015). The exactness of AR-enabled dental implant positioning was evaluated and analyzed by Lin, Yau, Wang, Zheng, and Chung (2015). Positioning was found to reduce placement deviations. The AR automation in dental implantology is cost-effective and has the ability to cut down factors like time and other costs (Ewers et al., 2005). Integration of knowledge and clinical skills along with problem-solving capabilities is a complicated task in dental education. Technological advancements are expected to change clinical dental teaching. The self-assessment and self-learning process with the pedagogic tools aids the apprentices to figure out the concepts clearly (Duta et al., 2011). Applying VR and AR for dental tutoring and training assists in simulating 3D practical procedures. Unrestricted access to practical sessions, quick learning feedback, and consistent assessment skills are supported by the AR systems (Schonwetter, Reynolds, Eaton, & De Vries, 2010). The simulation technology for training and valuation has increased greatly (Barry Issenberg, Mcgaghie, Petrusa, Lee Gordon, & Scalese, 2005). The use of AR systems to provide high-quality training, increase attention, and minimize hardware and software costs are some of the influences of the novel simulation technology in dental education and dental curricula (Haden et al., 2010).

The ultimate goal is to boost the value of dental education (Eaton, Reynolds, Grayden, & Wilson, 2008). The various VR dental simulators for training systems are PerioSim (Luciano, Banerjee, & DeFanti, 2009), HapTEL (San Diego et al., 2012), and VirDenT system (Corneliu, Mihaela, Mircea-Dorin, Crenguta, & Mircea, 2011).

BodyExplorer simulator uses AR technology for self-learning, where a projector is fixed directly above a patient simulator to view the anatomy. Sensors are fixed in the physical body model to measure and provide feedback to the students. Flight simulators are used in training nurses during acute situations in actual aircraft. A helicopter was fixed on the flight simulator platform to display real-world views. It was created to replicate the brain as if the person was present in an actual airplane. vSim is a web-based virtual nursing simulator to practice cognitive skills (Foronda et al., 2017).

AR tools are applied in teaching the framework of heart and bones and for interaction with the patients, trainees, and other physician's 3D printed models. Its presence is notable in anatomy training, preoperative surgery planning, intraoperative navigation, stroke recovery therapy, pain control management, laparoscopic surgery, eye-tracking technology, real-time holographic visualization, and simulation of emergency rescue operations for children and adults (Uppot et al., 2019).

8.4 Conclusion and Future Scope

AR is a fascinating concept and is cutting-edge technology. Smart AR technology is framing the future and is implemented in numerous industries. The use of smart components like cameras, sensors, and display devices that are wearable on the head and hand is creating a novel world. AR software collaborates with users every time to access digital information from the virtual and real world. It is essential to adopt AR in the medical sector as it offers various benefits to researchers, patients, doctors, nurses, radiologists, and pharmacists.

Any novel technology will have its advantages and disadvantages. It is necessary to understand the challenges of the AR system in healthcare. Handling voluminous data in the distributed network is a challenging task. One of the key concepts of AR is to combine users across the world in a virtual environment and provide them the facility to use the AR system. To model a healthcare system in AR, the necessity is to integrate various domains such as mathematics, medicine, information technology (IT), and physics. The fabrication of high-quality 3D models to interact with and simulate objects in the factual world is challenging. The system requires minimalistic use of hardware to collaborate with 3D applications. Many hospitals lack the knowledge and digital skills to execute AR technology in the right way. Another huge challenge is the compatibility of machinery and software platforms in the factual world. There are many technical hurdles, and cost is yet another challenge. The lack of sufficient funds for AR research studies in healthcare is a setback. Various other issues in regulations, policies, and insurance exist. Medical professionals, patients, and other users must show readiness in adapting to the novel technology. Issues related to marketing and fear about the possible side effects on the patient require attention. The telemedicine theory offers users access to healthcare information over the internet, smart devices, and mobile phones. AR-enabled tools offer consultation regarding surgical procedures. They also enable collaboration with surgeons present in different places and time zones. The AR tools are highly complex and are used in training medical professionals. The learning experience using the AR system is efficient as it facilitates understanding complex concepts easily. Many AR apps are used in assisting medical practices by professionals as they aid in completing day-to-day tasks exactly. The apps are helpful in engaging patients to monitor their health. The AR apps create various business opportunities in the healthcare industry. Finally, the emerging AR technology in healthcare provides transparent diagnosis, painless and user-friendly treatment, easy access to healthcare information, and updating healthcare records. The use of an AR system to connect the remote monitoring devices aids in enhancing overall healthcare.

Notes

1. Working towards building a healthier India, https://www.investindia.gov.in/sector/healthcare [accessed on 18 November 2020].
2. Impact analysis of COVID-19 on Augmented Reality (AR) in healthcare market, https://www.researchdive.com/covid-19-insights/218/global-augmented-reality-ar-in-healthcare-market [accessed on 18 November 2020].
3. A Brief History of Augmented Reality (Future trends and impact), https://learn.g2.com/history-of-augmented-reality [accessed on 19 November 2020].
4. Using Augmented Reality in Healthcare, https://getreferralmd.com/2019/11/using-augmented-reality-in-healthcare [accessed on 19 November 2020].
5. Super Simple (yet effective) AR Apps and their successful entry in the world of Augmented Reality Healthcare Applications: Augrealitypedia, https://www.augrealitypedia.com/augmented-reality-healthcare-applications/ [accessed on 20 November 2020].
6. First ever Dental Augmented Reality app launched, https://bitemagazine.com.au/first-ever-dental-augmented-reality-app-launched/, [accessed on 20 November 2020].
7. Augmented Reality in pharma: From production to treating patients. https://nanobotmedical.com/augmented-reality-in-pharma-from-production-to-treating-patients/ [accessed on 20 November 2020].

8. The future of healthcare: Augmented Reality and Mixed Reality use cases in medicine, https://program-ace.com/blog/future-of-healthcare-5-ar-mr-use-cases-in-medicine/, [accessed on 20 November 2020].
9. AR experience to improve doctor–patient communication, https://uxdesign.cc/improving-doctor-patient-communication-with-ar-6d8d356beb67 [accessed on 20 November 2020].

References

Amini, S., & Kersten-Oertel, M. (2019). Augmented reality mastectomy surgical planning prototype using the HoloLens template for healthcare technology letters. *Healthcare Technology Letters, 6*(6), 261–265.

Barry Issenberg, S., Mcgaghie, W. C., Petrusa, E. R., Lee Gordon, D., & Scalese, R. J. (2005). Features and uses of high-fidelity medical simulations that lead to effective learning: A BEME systematic review. *Medical Teacher, 27*(1), 10–28.

Berryman, D. R. (2012). Augmented reality: A review. *Medical Reference Services Quarterly, 31*(2), 212–218.

Bork, F., Stratmann, L., Enssle, S., Eck, U., Navab, N., Waschke, J., & Kugelmann, D. (2019). The benefits of an augmented reality magic mirror system for integrated radiology teaching in gross anatomy. *Anatomical Sciences Education, 12*(6), 585–598.

Brunetti, P., Croatti, A., Ricci, A., & Viroli, M. (2015). Smart augmented fields for emergency operations. *Procedia Computer Science, 63*, 392–399.

Carlson, K. J., & Gagnon, D. J. (2016). Augmented reality integrated simulation education in health care. *Clinical Simulation in Nursing, 12*(4), 123–127.

Carmigniani, J., Furht, B., Anisetti, M., Ceravolo, P., Damiani, E., & Ivkovic, M. (2011). Augmented reality technologies, systems and applications. *Multimedia Tools and Applications, 51*(1), 341–377.

Corneliu, A., Mihaela, D., Mircea-Dorin, P., Crenguta, B., & Mircea, G. (2011, December). *Teeth reduction dental preparation using virtual and augmented reality by Constanta dental medicine students through the VirDenT system.* In the International Conference Development, Energy, Environment, Economics, Puerto De La Cruz, Tenerife, Spain.

Cui, N., Kharel, P., & Gruev, V. (2017, February). Augmented reality with Microsoft HoloLens holograms for near infrared fluorescence based image guided surgery. In *Molecular-guided surgery: Molecules, devices, and applications III* (Vol. 10049, p. 100490I). International Society for Optics and Photonics. SPIE BiOS, San Francisco, California, United States.

Dalgarno, B., & Lee, M. J. (2010). What are the learning affordances of 3-D virtual environments?. *British Journal of Educational Technology, 41*(1), 10–32.

Douglas, D. B., Wilke, C. A., Gibson, J. D., Boone, J. M., & Wintermark, M. (2017). Augmented reality: Advances in diagnostic imaging. *Multimodal Technologies and Interaction, 1*(4), 29.

Duta, M., Amariei, C. I., Bogdan, C. M., Popovici, D. M., Ionescu, N., & Nuca, C. I. (2011). An overview of virtual and augmented reality in dental education. *Oral Health and Dental Management, 10*, 42–49.

Eaton, K. A., Reynolds, P. A., Grayden, S. K., & Wilson, N. H. F. (2008). A vision of dental education in the third millennium. *British Dental Journal, 205*(5), 261–271.

El-Hariri, H., Pandey, P., Hodgson, A. J., & Garbi, R. (2018). Augmented reality visualisation for orthopedic surgical guidance with pre-and intra-operative multimodal image data fusion. *Healthcare Technology Letters, 5*(5), 189–193.

Ewers, R., Schicho, K., Undt, G., Wanschitz, F., Truppe, M., Seemann, R., & Wagner, A. (2005). Basic research and 12 years of clinical experience in computer-assisted navigation technology: A review. *International Journal of Oral and Maxillofacial Surgery, 34*(1), 1–8.

Fida, B., Cutolo, F., di Franco, G., Ferrari, M., & Ferrari, V. (2018). Augmented reality in open surgery. *Updates in Surgery, 70*(3), 389–400.

Foronda, C. L., Alfes, C. M., Dev, P., Kleinheksel, A. J., Nelson Jr, D. A., O'Donnell, J. M., & Samosky, J. T. (2017). Virtually nursing: Emerging technologies in nursing education. *Nurse Educator, 42*(1), 14–17.

Forrest, W. P., Mackey, M. A., Shah, V. M., Hassell, K. M., Shah, P., Wylie, J. L., … & Helmy, R. (2017). Mixed reality meets pharmaceutical development. *Journal of Pharmaceutical Sciences, 106*(12), 3438–3441.

Gavaghan, K. A., Peterhans, M., Oliveira-Santos, T., & Weber, S. (2011). A portable image overlay projection device for computer-aided open liver surgery. *IEEE Transactions on Biomedical Engineering, 58*(6), 1855–1864.

Haden, N. K., Hendricson, W. D., Kassebaum, D. K., Ranney, R. R., Weinstein, G., Anderson, E. L., & Valachovic, R. W. (2010). Curriculum change in dental education, 2003–09. *Journal of Dental Education, 74*(5), 539–557.

Herron, J. (2016). Augmented reality in medical education and training. *Journal of Electronic Resources in Medical Libraries, 13*(2), 51–55.

Izard, S. G., Mendez, J. A. J., Ruisoto, P., & Garcia-Penalvo, F. J. (2018, October). *NextMed: How to enhance 3D radiological images with Augmented and Virtual Reality.* In Proceedings of theSixth International Conference on Technological Ecosystems for Enhancing Multiculturality (pp. 397–404).

Katic, D., Spengler, P., Bodenstedt, S., Castrillon-Oberndorfer, G., Seeberger, R., Hoffmann, J., & Speidel, S. (2015). A system for context-aware intraoperative augmented reality in dental implant surgery. *International Journal of Computer Assisted Radiology and Surgery, 10*(1), 101–108.

Kobayashi, L., Zhang, X. C., Collins, S. A., Karim, N., & Merck, D. L. (2018). Exploratory application of augmented reality/mixed reality devices for acute care procedure training. *Western Journal of Emergency Medicine, 19*(1), 158.

Kwon, H. B., Park, Y. S., & Han, J. S. (2018). Augmented reality in dentistry: A current perspective. *Acta Odontologica Scandinavica, 76*(7), 497–503.

Lee, Y., & Lee, C. H. (2018). Augmented reality for personalized nanomedicines. *Biotechnology Advances, 36*(1), 335–343.

Leger, E., Drouin, S., Collins, D. L., Popa, T., & Kersten-Oertel, M. (2017). Quantifying attention shifts in augmented reality image-guided neurosurgery. *Healthcare Technology Letters, 4*(5), 188–192.

Lin, Y. K., Yau, H. T., Wang, I. C., Zheng, C., & Chung, K. H. (2015). A novel dental implant guided surgery based on integration of surgical template and augmented reality. *Clinical Implant Dentistry and Related Research, 17*(3), 543–553.

Lovo, E. E., Quintana, J. C., Puebla, M. C., Torrealba, G., Santos, J. L., Lira, I. H., & Tagle, P. (2007). A novel, inexpensive method of image coregistration for applications in image-guided surgery using augmented reality. *Operative Neurosurgery, 60*(suppl_4), 366.

Luciano, C., Banerjee, P., & DeFanti, T. (2009). Haptics-based virtual reality periodontal training simulator. *Virtual Reality, 13*(2), 69–85.

McCarthy, C. J., Alvin, Y. C., Do, S., Dawson, S. L., & Uppot, R. N. (2018). Interventional radiology training using a dynamic medical immersive training environment (DynaMITE). *Journal of the American College of Radiology, 15*(5), 789–793.

Monge, J., & Postolache, O. (2018, October). *Augmented reality and smart sensors for physical rehabilitation.* In 2018 International Conference and Exposition on Electrical and Power Engineering (EPE) (pp. 1010–1014). IEEE.

Moreta-Martinez, R., García-Mato, D., García-Sevilla, M., Pérez-Mañanes, R., Calvo-Haro, J., & Pascau, J. (2018). Augmented reality in computer-assisted interventions based on patient-specific 3D printed references. *Healthcare Technology Letters, 5*(5), 162–166.

Ponce, B. A., Menendez, M. E., Oladeji, L. O., Fryberger, C. T., & Dantuluri, P. K. (2014). Emerging technology in surgical education: Combining real-time augmented reality and wearable computing devices. *Orthopedics, 37*(11), 751–757.

San Diego, J. P., Cox, M. J., Quinn, B. F., Newton, J. T., Banerjee, A., & Woolford, M. (2012). Researching haptics in higher education: The complexity of developing haptics virtual learning systems and evaluating its impact on students' learning. *Computers & Education, 59*(1), 156–166.

Sayadi, L. R., Naides, A., Eng, M., Fijany, A., Chopan, M., Sayadi, J. J., & Widgerow, A. D. (2019). The new frontier: A review of augmented reality and virtual reality in plastic surgery. *Aesthetic Surgery Journal, 39*(9), 1007–1016.

Schonwetter, D. J., Reynolds, P. A., Eaton, K. A., & De Vries, J. (2010). Online learning in dentistry: An overview of the future direction for dental education. *Journal of Oral Rehabilitation, 37*(12), 927–940.

Sirilak, S., & Muneesawang, P. (2018). A new procedure for advancing telemedicine using HoloLens. *IEEE Access, 6*, 60224–60233.

Smorodin, G., Kolesnichenko, O., Kolesnichenko, Y., Myakinkova, L., Prisyazhnaya, N., Yakovleva, D., & Litvak, N. (2017, November). *Internet of things: Modem paradigm of health care.* In 2017 21st Conference of Open Innovations Association (FRUCT) (pp. 311–320). IEEE.

Uppot, R. N., Laguna, B., McCarthy, C. J., De Novi, G., Phelps, A., Siegel, E., & Courtier, J. (2019). Implementing virtual and augmented reality tools for radiology education and training, communication, and clinical care. *Radiology, 291*(3), 570–580.

Vavra, P., Roman, J., Zonca, P., Ihnát, P., Němec, M., Kumar, J., & El-Gendi, A. (2017). Recent development of augmented reality in surgery: A review. *Journal of Healthcare Engineering, 2017.* pp. 1–9.

Verhey, J. T., Haglin, J. M., Verhey, E. M., & Hartigan, D. E. (2020). Virtual, augmented, and mixed reality applications in orthopedic surgery. *The International Journal of Medical Robotics and Computer Assisted Surgery, 16*(2), e2067.

Zhu, E., Hadadgar, A., Masiello, I., & Zary, N. (2014). Augmented reality in healthcare education: An integrative review. *PeerJ, 2*, e469.

Zhu, M., Liu, F., Chai, G., Pan, J. J., J iang, T., Lin, L., & Li, Q. (2017). A novel augmented reality system for displaying inferior alveolar nerve bundles in maxillofacial surgery. *Scientific Reports, 7*, 42365.

Appendix

Abbreviations

AI: Artificial intelligence
AR: Augmented reality
ARML: Augmented reality markup language
CRT: Cathode-ray tube
GPS: Global positioning system
HMD: Head-mounted display
HUD: Heads-up display technology
ICT: Information and communication technology
KG: Kindergarten
LED: Light-emitting diode
MOOC: Massive Open Online Course
PG: Post-graduate
OER: Open educational resources
OGC: Open geospatial consortium
RFID: Radio-frequency identification
SAR: Spatial augmented reality
SDK: Software development kit
SPOC: Small private online course
STEM: Science, technology, engineering, and mathematics
VRD: Virtual retinal display
SLAM: Simultaneous localization and mapping
MEMS: Micro-electromechanical system
XML: Extensible markup language
VR: Virtual reality

Index

Note: *Italicized* page numbers refer to figures, **bold** page numbers refer to tables

CPSIA information can be obtained
at www.ICGtesting.com
Printed in the USA
BVHW050451110522
636361BV00002B/28